Project Management Competence

Project Management Competence

Building Key Skills for Individuals, Teams, and Organizations

J. Davidson Frame

Jossey-Bass Publishers • San Francisco

Jossey-Bass books and products are available through most bookstores. To contact Jossey-Bass directly, call (888) 378–2537, fax to (800) 605–2665, or visit our website at www.josseybass.com.

Substantial discounts on bulk quantities of Jossey-Bass books are available to corporations, professional associations, and other organizations. For details and discount information, contact the special sales department at Jossey-Bass.

 Manufactured in the United States of America on Lyons Falls Turin Book. This paper is acid-free and 100 percent totally chlorine-free.

Library of Congress Cataloging-in-Publication Data

Frame, J. Davidson.
   Project management competence : building key skills for individuals, teams, and organizations / J. Davidson Frame.
     p.   cm. — (The Jossey-Bass business & management series)
   Includes bibliographical references and index.
   ISBN 0-7879-4662-1
   1. Industrial project management.   I. Title.   II. Series.
HD69.P75F733   1999
658.4'04—dc21

                         99-31823

FIRST EDITION
HB Printing 10 9 8 7 6 5 4 3 2 1

The Jossey-Bass
Business & Management Series

Contents

This book is dedicated to my wife, Yanping

Preface

From 1990 to 1995, I directed the Project Management Institute's (PMI) project management certification program. When I began the job, I did not realize that it would occupy me seven days a week, fifty-two weeks a year for six years.

During this time I was immersed in the issue of competence. At first my mission seemed pretty straightforward: I should work with my colleagues at PMI to develop an exam that assessed the knowledge-based competencies of project professionals. We had guidance on what project management competencies are through PMI's *Guide to the Project Management Body of Knowledge* (PMBOK) (Duncan, 1996), a "bible" of knowledge areas that project professionals should master. My job was to figure out how to measure these competencies. The principal challenge appeared to be to write good exam questions and to come up with meaningful multiple-choice responses.

As time went by, I learned that things were not so simple. The intricacies of competency began to reveal themselves. I received five to twenty phone calls each day, seven days a week, from all manner of people: individual project workers, training directors, PMI officers, PMI chapter members, corporate vice presidents, presidents, newspaper reporters, magazine writers, representatives of international project groups, and members of trade associations. These people came from a myriad of industries and disciplines: civil engineering, finance, information technology, education and training, telecommunications, oil recovery, environmental cleanup, pharmaceuticals, school administration, facilities management, transportation, defense, and state and local government. As I talked to all of these people, I came to see that there are many perspectives on what constitutes project management competence. Some people view it narrowly; to them, project management competence entails mastering the basic skills of scheduling, budgeting, and resource allocation. Others view it broadly; to them, competence incorporates a whole range of social and business skills in addition to the traditional knowledge-based skills associated with project management.

As I was running PMI's certification program, I was also teaching graduate courses in organizational management, conducting research on assorted project management topics, and working with a wide array of companies and government agencies, including AT&T, NCR, Lucent Technologies, IBM, GTE Internetworking (BBN), Motorola, EDS, Citibank, Philip Morris, Perot Systems, Nokia, Asea Brown Boveri, the federal courts, the Internal Revenue Service, the China State Shipbuilding Corporation, the Executive Office of the President, and the Defense Systems Management College. Through my work it became obvious to me that even the most competent individuals in the world are going to have a tough time achieving their project objectives if they are members of mediocre teams and if they do not get the materials and moral support they need from their organizations. So project management competence entails more than developing qualified people (which is the principal focus of the PMI certification effort).

The key theme of this book is that achieving project management competence entails the concurrent development of individual competence, team competence, and organizational competence. In this book I describe what each of these types of competence means and provide a mechanism to assess whether they are being achieved.

Intended Audience

As I describe the intended audience for this book it is tempting to point to anyone who plans to work in knowledge-based organizations during the next few decades, because it has become obvious that organizing knowledge work along project lines has become the central way of doing business everywhere. Although I am convinced that such a description is appropriate, my editor has asked whether I could be a bit more focused, so here goes.

This book is written primarily for two audiences: those who desire to *strengthen* their project management competence and those who wish to *assess* the project management competence of individuals, teams, and organizations. Let's look at each audience in turn.

Those who desire to strengthen their project management competence are men and women working in a broad range of fields where project management has assumed critical importance. Included here are people working in traditional project-focused arenas, such as construction and the defense sectors; those in the hot, emerging high-tech areas, such as information technology, telecommunications, and research and development; and those operating in areas that are just discovering the power of project management, such as finance, marketing and sales, real estate development, and training.

Men and women in these areas agree with *Fortune* magazine, which stated in 1995 that project management has become a career path of choice (Stewart, 1995b). These people realize that in an era of organizational flattening, reengineering, empowerment, and outsourcing, project management provides one of the few opportunities for individuals to move ahead.

Those who desire to assess the project management competence of individuals, teams, and organizations are typically people who want to make project management work in their organizations. They recognize that effective project operations require competence at the level of individuals, teams, and the overall organization. They should find this book useful because it provides the foundation for conducting such assessments. Not only does the book describe the meaning of project management competence at the level of individuals, teams, and organizations, but it also supplies diagnostic tools to assess competence at these different levels.

Contents of the Book

The book is divided into four parts. Part One comprises three chapters, each of which explores broad issues of project management competence. Chapter One examines why the issue of competence is so important today. It posits that project competence must be approached from a three-pronged perspective: from the viewpoints of individuals, teams, and organizations. It poses the "competence dilemma," which has its origins in the conflict between the theoretical view that all people are competent if given proper support and the reality of great variations in individual capabilities. Chapter Two looks at the connection between competence and rewards. A review of the economics of competence shows that the most competent performers add far more value than average or subaverage performers. Consequently, the rewards that competent performers garner are high. The chapter also explores the idea that in today's brutally competitive world competence is our sword and shield, enabling us to survive the tribulations of downsizing, flattening, and reengineering. Chapter Three raises the point that competence cannot be nurtured in sick organizations. When such phenomena as selfishness, organizational defense routines, dysfunctional cultures, and corruption prevail, competence withers. A variety of commonly encountered pathologies are explored.

Part Two comprises five chapters, each of which examines different aspects of the competence of individual people functioning in project environments. Chapter Four reviews the key traits found in the most effective project professionals. It also itemizes the competencies defined in *Guide to the PMBOK* and presents a checklist of project management tools that competent project professionals should master. Chapter Five explores how people can strengthen their project management knowledge base through a variety of channels, ranging from formal education to on-the-job training to self-instruction. The chapter emphasizes that in the final analysis mastery of project management knowledge will be derived not from books but rather from continual practice. Chapter Six looks at the role that so-called people skills play in project management. Projects seldom fail because a PERT system crashes; however, they often fail because key team members lack good people skills. In particular, the chapter stresses that effective project professionals must develop solid empathy and intrapersonal relations capabilities. Other soft skills examined include political skills, team-building skills, listening skills, and communication skills.

Chapter Seven highlights the need for project professionals to possess both good business sense and business knowledge. Project management has moved away from the position that project professionals are mere implementers of technical solutions. Today they are expected to have broad business insights. They need these insights to run their projects. They also need them so that they can communicate effectively with their customers, many of whom expect business solutions to their problems. The chapter contains a checklist of business skills that effective project professionals should possess. Chapter Eight offers readers a multiple-choice assessment tool, fashioned roughly after PMI's certification exam. Questions are asked in eight PMBOK knowledge areas so that readers can assess their mastery of project-related knowledge area by area.

Part Three consists of two chapters. Chapter Nine examines what teams are, what they do, and why they are so important in today's competitive and complex world. Various team structures are reviewed in detail, including matrix-based teams, self-managed teams, and co-responsibility teams. Chapter Ten establishes criteria for effective teams and develops a methodology for assessing team competence on the basis of these criteria. The chapter also provides a team competence assessment instrument.

Part Four also consists of two chapters. Chapter Eleven provides a seven-element framework for identifying the key traits of organizational competence in project-based organizations. It emphasizes that the distinguishing feature of the most competent organizations is that they provide their teams and individuals with the support they need to do their jobs effectively. Chapter Twelve offers a scoring checklist that readers can employ to assess the degree to which their organizations provide an environment that enables teams and individuals to operate effectively, and it describes the key traits of two popular approaches to assessing organizational competence: the ISO 9000 and the Software Engineering Institute's Capability Maturity Model.

The Conclusion wraps up the principal themes of the book.

A Word of Thanks

This book is the result of my interactions with literally thousands of people. Most of these people have been students: in executive development seminars; in the classrooms at George Washington University, where I taught from 1979 until 1998; or at my new home at the University of Management and Technology. These students have provided me with invaluable insights into what they have experienced in their organizations. They have also tolerated my attempts to test new ideas on them. Their responses to my "experiments" have helped me to develop a good sense of which ideas work and which do not.

I have also received valuable insights through my dealings with training directors and senior project managers in many organizations, including Charles Georghiou at SITA; Sherry Higgins at

Lucent Technologies; Ernie Waldstein at the Australia Graduate School of Management; Gus Crosetto and David Suh at Fannie Mae; Thomas Block at the University of Management and Technology; Simon Indola at Nokia; Luis Herrera at Hoffman-LaRoche; Kenneth Fuller and George Pico at Citibank; Richard Howarth at Alcatel Submarine Networks; Nicholas Schacht, Leroy Ward, and Carl Pritchard at ESI; Thomas Tarnow at Morgan Stanley; Richard Humphrey at Westinghouse; Lele Wang at Procter and Gamble; and William Bahnmaier at the Defense Systems Management College. This is only a partial list of people who have helped me develop my ideas. When I think of all the people who have openly and generously shared their views with me, I am nearly overwhelmed.

Very special thanks go to my editor at Jossey-Bass, Cedric Crocker, who I used for frequent sanity checks to make sure I was on track in my writing. Sometimes I began to drift a bit and he set me straight. His suggestions had a substantial impact on the direction the book took, and I firmly believe that whatever strengths the book has owe a strong debt to him.

Special thanks also go to my wife, Yanping Chen, who I can honestly say is one of the most effective business managers I have ever encountered—and she is a project manager to boot! She bore with me during the four years it took to write this book (and also tolerated my moods while I wrote two preceding books) and provided many insights that I incorporated. I dedicate this book to her.

Finally, I thank my daughter, Katherine, whose support I first acknowledged five books ago when she was just three years old. At that time I thanked her for not pulling the plug on my word processor, a tempting prospect for any three-year-old. Today she is eighteen and has her own word processor, and my thanks are directed at all the pleasure she gives me through her keen intelligence, thoughtfulness, beautiful singing voice, and most especially her wicked sense of humor.

Arlington, Virginia
May 1999

J. DAVIDSON FRAME

The Author

J. DAVIDSON FRAME is professor and dean of academic affairs at the newly created University of Management and Technology, a graduate university focusing on the management of projects, technology, telecommunications, information technology, and risk. From 1979 until 1998, he was on the faculty of The George Washington University (GWU), where he served as chairman of the Department of Management Science; director of the Program on Science, Technology, and Innovation; and director of the International Center for Project Management Excellence. He established GWU's master of science degree program in project management, which grew within two years to be the world's largest program of its type.

Prior to joining the GWU faculty, Frame was vice president at Computer Horizons, where he led some thirty projects involving software development and quantitative model building. From 1990 to 1995, Frame was director of certification at the Project Management Institute (PMI), the world's largest society of project professionals. From 1996 through 1998 he was PMI's director of educational services.

Frame has consulted with and trained executives at many organizations, including AT&T, Lucent Technologies, NCR, SITA, Fannie Mae, Freddie Mac, Asea Brown Boveri, IBM, Motorola, GTE Internetworking (BBN), 3M, Fidia Pharmaceuticals, CUNA Mutual, China State Shipbuilding Corporation, Chinese Academy of Sciences, the Executive Office of the President, the federal courts, the Internal Revenue Service, the Army Corps of Engineers, the Defense Information Systems Agency, the Australia Graduate School of Management, the Korean Industrial Technology Agency, the World Bank, and the United Nations. Since 1983 he has trained an estimated twenty thousand executives in the areas of project management, risk management, technology transfer, and technology management.

Frame has authored six books and more than forty scholarly articles. He received his bachelor's degree from the College of Wooster (1967) and his doctorate from the School of International Service at the American University (1976).

Project Management Competence

Part One

Project Management Competence for the Successful Organization

Chapter One

Developing Project-Competent Organizations

One should not worry about the fact that other people do not appreciate one. One should worry about the fact that one is incapable.
Confucius, *ANALECTS,* BOOK 14, CH. 30

Increasingly, businesses, governments, and nonprofit organizations are consciously organizing their activities as projects. Of course there is nothing new about undertaking projects in organizations. Anyone who doubts this need merely visit Machu Picchu in the Andes or the Hangzhou canal in China or the Colosseum in Rome. What is new is the deliberation with which projects are being introduced and executed today. In many organizations, projects have become the central focus of management activity, whereas until quite recently they lay at the periphery of the organization's core efforts.

At the same time that projects have moved to the forefront of human activity, there has been a parallel heightened focus on identifying and developing competence in organizations. Increasingly managers and workers are asking questions such as, What skills should we possess in order to do the job? Do we have them? How can we acquire them? As with projects, concern with competence is not new. Military commanders have discussed its importance for millennia. It was a major topic in Plato's *Republic*. It has long served as good source material for humorists; consider how many of the tales in *Aesop's Fables,* developed 2,600 years ago, contrast competent with incompetent behavior. As with projects, what is new is the deliberation with which competence is being identified and sought.

These two forces—the conscious drives to organize work as projects and to identify and pursue competence in the workplace—are merging, and they form the central topic of this book. Their common denominator can be stated in a single word: *competition.* Competition lies at the root of the astonishing management transformations we are experiencing today. Outsourcing, flattening, reengineering, Total Quality Management, empowerment, and the myriad of other management methods that people are experimenting with today are all attempts to create organizations that can produce goods and services faster, cheaper, and better in order to gain or maintain markets.

A well-known example of how projects can form the nucleus of business activity is seen in the development of the IBM personal computer (PC) at the end of the 1970s. To bypass IBM's oppressive bureaucratic processes, the PC project was located outside of the organization's mainstream operations. The project team was situated in a leaky warehouse in Boca Raton, Florida. The PC team basically functioned as an independent business unit.

The success of the IBM PC project became the stuff of business legend. The project team produced a product that would revolutionize how organizations do business—and it did this in record-breaking time. It even spawned a great software company when it decided to base the PC's operating system on a product offered by a tiny unknown company called Microsoft. The success of the IBM PC in the marketplace was far greater than business forecasters had anticipated, and the resulting shortage of PCs in the market enabled a start-up clone maker—Compaq—to have the fastest growth of sales of a business start-up in business history—from zero dollars to one billion dollars of revenue in one year! Ultimately, IBM's PC produced a multibillion-dollar business for IBM, and helped launch a huge industry—*from what began as a relatively innocuous project.*

Of course IBM is not the only organization that has built a business around a project. 3M is well known for operating in this fashion. One way to get ahead in the company is to sign onto a project that ultimately leads to the creation of a highly successful product. Successful projects lead to the creation of new divisions at 3M, and key project players often play a significant role in these new divisions.

Pharmaceutical companies also build businesses from projects. A research and development (R&D) project might lead to the development of a promising new drug. Then the drug must go through a lengthy regulatory review (in the United States this entails review by the Food and Drug Administration). Interestingly, the regulatory review effort itself is generally organized as a project by the pharmaceutical companies. Once a drug has regulatory approval, it becomes the basis of a new business.

The list goes on. Well-known organizations that owe their existence to the implementation of successful projects include Apple Computer, Oracle, Netscape, and Lotus, as well as a host of biotech companies, such as Genentech, Cetus, and Medimmune.

By the late 1990s, project management had become a hot topic. Management gurus such as Tom Peters were hailing its value. Business writers such as *Fortune*'s Tom Stewart were identifying it as a key to survival and success in today's chaotic business environment (Stewart, 1995a, 1995b). Membership in project management societies experienced exponential growth; for example, membership in the Project Management Institute grew from twelve thousand members in 1994 to forty thousand in 1998.

In this environment that focused on the importance of project management, some very significant institutional players took steps to implement project management theory and practice systematically, including AT&T, Asea Brown Boveri, IBM, Citibank, Motorola, Hewlett-Packard, EDS, Fannie Mae, Freddie Mac, Korea's PROMAT, Bell South, Bellcore, Nynex, Bell Atlantic, U.S. West, the Army Corps of Engineers, and the Defense Systems Management College. These and other organizations began sending legions of employees to project management training courses, purchasing large volumes of project scheduling software, and reengineering their business operations to accommodate the new look of project management.

As more and more organizations launched initiatives to adopt project management perspectives and methodologies in their operations, they began to ask a number of important questions: Are our project management development efforts focusing on the right issues? Are our people developing the right skills? Are we configuring our project management efforts in the right way? Underlying these questions was the realization that to employ project management effectively we must know how to identify project management competencies.

This is not a trivial issue. As this book makes clear, commitment to implementing project management best practices means that organizations must be willing to delegate decision-making authority to project teams. Thus the organization's health—indeed, its very existence—depends increasingly on decisions made in a decentralized fashion. Naturally, significant questions arise about the capabilities of the decentralized decision makers and the capacity of the organization to foster an environment that leads to good decision making. Key questions include the following:

- How capable are *individuals* at identifying and implementing solutions to problems?
- How effective are *teams* at harnessing the cross-functional perspectives needed to resolve complex problems in a messy world?
- How capable are *organizations* at creating an environment that enables individuals and teams to carry out their jobs effectively?

Three Levels of Project Competence

These questions suggest that project management competence must be reviewed on three levels: the individual, the team, and the organization.

Individual Competence

The competence of individuals is addressed when we raise the question, How capable are the people working on the project? On a typical project there are five broad categories of project players: the project manager, the sponsor, technical personnel, functional managers overseeing the efforts of the technical personnel, and support staff. If any of these individuals is weak, the project is in jeopardy. To see why this is true, consider the roles played by each of these individuals.

Project manager. Project managers bear ultimate responsibility for making things happen. Traditionally they have carried out this role as mere implementers. To do their jobs they needed to have basic administrative and technical competencies. Today they play a far broader role. In addition to the traditional skills, they need to have business skills, customer relations skills, and political skills. Psychologically, they must be results-oriented self-starters with a high tolerance for ambiguity, because little is clear-cut in today's tumultuous business environment. Shortcomings in any of these areas can lead to project failure.

An interesting development to watch is the recent shift from a focus on project managers per se to the use of two or more people in carrying out the project management function. For example, in the early 1990s the Administrative Office of the U.S. Courts began dividing the project management function between two players: a *development manager* concerned with technical issues and what can be termed a *business manager* concerned with nontechnical aspects of running a project. These two individuals collectively serve as the project manager. Alcatel Submarine Systems created a similar decision-making structure but with three people. NCR went beyond this and created Customer Focus Teams, units of four or five people (such as from sales, information technology, engineering, and finance) who collectively carry out the project management function. As this trend grows, it will be interesting to see whether people in organizations continue to talk about the project manager as the key individual responsible for enabling projects to achieve their goals.

Project sponsor. Project sponsors are often needed to create an environment that enables the project team to do its job effectively. Typically they are powerful people in the organization who have a measure of control over resources. It is their job to protect the team from organizational distractions, such as political game playing and bureaucratic nit-picking. In addition, they must use their clout to make sure that the team receives the resources it needs to achieve its objectives. Broadly speaking, the key competencies desired of project sponsors include the effective use of power, the capacity to obtain needed resources quickly, and the ability to influence important organizational players to support the project. Clearly, project sponsors whose key competencies are weak will hinder the successful achievement of project objectives.

Technical personnel. Technical personnel are the shock troops of the project team. They do the work that leads to the production of the deliverable. On software projects, they design systems and write and test the software code; on construction projects, they develop the architectural drawings, order materials, and build the structure; on pharmaceutical projects, they conduct the R&D that leads to the development of new drugs and carry out the clinical trials that result in regulatory approval. In a sense the competencies of technical personnel are the easiest to measure. Good software programmers, designers, and clinicians are fairly easy to spot. They produce their work faster, better, and cheaper than their colleagues. A project implemented by mediocre technical personnel is a project doomed to failure.

Functional managers. Functional managers are the men and women who control the resources that are employed on projects. They include such players as the director of information systems, the chief of systems testers, the head of maintenance, and the director of marketing. Competencies sought in these people include the ability to plan resource allocations effectively and the capacity to meet their commitments. Functional managers who supply the project team with the right resources at the right time contribute to project success. Those who do not contribute to project failure.

Support staff. Projects depend heavily on cooperation from support staff, including accountants, budgeters, purchasing agents, scheduling personnel, legal personnel, and clerical staff. Clearly projects that are supported by staff who are competent in their jobs have a higher probability of success than projects that are not.

Team Competence

It is not enough to have highly capable people assigned to a project. For the project to succeed, these people must work together as a team. That is, they must recognize that they are addressing a common goal, and they must be willing and able to work together to achieve it.

Teams form the basic work units of projects. One of the major trends in management practice today is recognition that our complex and messy business environment requires team-based solutions to problems. An advantage of teams is that they provide us with cross-functional insights into possible project solutions. Increasingly the problems we face demand cross-functional solutions. Before building a deliverable, we need to know whether it has a market, whether it can be built cost-effectively, whether it can be operated and maintained once the project is finished, and so on. Answers to these significant questions can best be gained by placing representatives from the marketing department, operations department, and maintenance department onto the project team.

Organizational Competence

Some organizations clearly foster competence while others seem hell-bent on promoting incompetence. Competence-focused organizations support their workers in carrying out their jobs as effectively as possible. Organizations do this by creating an environment that encourages collaboration, by supplying their workers with the resources necessary to operate effectively, and by sustaining an infrastructure that offers their employees the information they need to do their jobs properly.

In recent years, the quality movement has directed a good deal of attention onto organizations and their role in promoting effective work efforts. In Europe, the ISO 9000 quality initiative concentrated its attention on determining whether organizations implement consistent processes that lead to the production of high-quality goods and services. In the United States, the Malcolm Baldrige Award and in Japan the Deming Prize similarly examine the organization's efforts to promote the production of high-quality goods and services. Perhaps the most sophisticated attempt at assessing organizational competence has been carried out by Carnegie Mellon University's Software Engineering Institute, which is the sponsor of the Capability Maturity Model for determining whether organizations have created support systems that encourage the development of high-quality software.

What Is Competence?

The word *competence* comes from the Latin *competens*, which is the present participle of the verb *competere*. This verb consists of two parts: *com*, which means "together," and *petere*, which means "to strive." Thus *competere* literally means "to strive together." Interestingly, the words *competence* and *competition* are both derived from *competere;* and as we have seen, competition is the driving force behind the current focus on competence.

The idea of competence is closely associated with the idea of capability. Competent people are capable people, just as competent teams are capable teams, and competent organizations are capable organizations. This association with capability suggests that competence is concerned with getting the job done. In the context of today's management terminology, competence is about *adding value.*

Humans have been concerned with competence for millennia. In his *Republic,* Plato devotes a substantial number of words to describing the traits of the *philosopher king,* a supercompetent individual who should be entrusted with governing a society. In his *Analects,* Plato's Chinese contemporary Confucius makes it clear that competent people are special and that achieving competence should be a prime goal of the *sage* (*zhun* in Mandarin; can also be translated as "gentleman," a thoughtful person who stands at the pinnacle of society's elite). In a similar vein, the Hebrew Bible is filled with stories glorifying competent men and women and demeaning incompetent fools.

More recently, management theorists and practitioners have focused on the importance of competence in what has become known as the competency movement. In a nutshell, the competency movement addresses two questions: What should we be good at? and What steps should we take to develop these prescribed competencies? The competency movement received enormous attention with the publication of C. K. Prahalad and Gary Hamel's 1990 article "The Core Competence of the Organization" in the *Harvard Business Review.*

Prahalad and Hamel maintain that the organizations that will survive and thrive in these turbulent times are those that nurture their core competencies. These core competencies possess three characteristics: first, they make a disproportionate contribution to customer-perceived value; second, they differentiate an organization from its competitors, making it something special; and finally, they offer what Prahalad and Hamel call *extendability*—that is, they strengthen capabilities that will enable the organization to thrive in the future.

For the purposes of this book, *competence* is defined simply. I take my cue from William James (1907), whose philosophy of pragmatism was based on the following proposition: in the final analysis, it is results that count. The defining characteristic of competent individuals, teams, and organizations is that *they consistently produce desired results.* They deliver the goods—on time, within budget, and according to specifications, and they do this in such a way as to maximize customers' delight.

While the basic proposition is simple, its implications are not. For individuals, teams, and organizations to deliver the goods, they must possess threshold levels of pertinent education, a track record of experience in operating effectively, and support systems that enable capable people to reach their potential. In addition, they must adhere to values that promote innovation, intelligent risk taking, and openness. Both the individuals associated with teams and the organization must possess a drive to succeed and a deep-seated sense of accountability. (There is no room for buck passers on projects!)

The Competence Dilemma

There are wide variations in the ability of individuals, teams, and organizations to carry out their work. This is a difficult reality to digest for some men and women who live in liberal democracies. A fundamental operating premise of liberal democracies is that people are equal and must be treated as such. This view is even codified in the opening words of one of the great documents of history, the American *Declaration of Independence,* whose preamble states, "We hold these truths to be self-evident, that all men are created equal."

This is a wise principle for governments to hold. Its adoption for the governance of the United States has contributed mightily to the success of the American democratic experiment. Consider the opposing principle: "We hold these truths to be self-evident, *that all men are created unequal.*" Societies that hold this perspective can use it to rationalize formal class systems, the extreme version of which is a caste system. Such systems are the antithesis of meritocracy. People are valued not according to their ability but according to the class into which they are born. Ultimately, class systems work against rewarding competence.

Although effective governments have reason to treat their citizens as equal, it is nonetheless clear that the capabilities of people vary dramatically. This can be seen in a simple example. If five people are each given the task of making a wooden box from a given supply of materials using the same set of tools, some individuals will finish the job far more quickly than others. Furthermore, the quality of the resulting boxes will vary dramatically from individual to individual.

What holds for the construction of boxes also holds for the writing of software code, the design of buildings, the drafting of user manuals, the soldering of circuits, and the delivery of a good speech. The fact is that different people possess divergent capabilities to do their jobs. Their capabilities are determined by a variety of factors, including their interest in doing the job, their experience in performing similar work in the past, their formal training, and their commitment to doing good work.

The competence dilemma is this: although our hearts tell us that the people with whom we work in our organizations should be treated as equals, our heads tell us that in the realm of work they are not equals. Some people add far more value to an organization's operations than others. In fact, experience suggests that those who add the most value are a small fraction of the workforce. When it comes to competence, the 80–20 rule appears to hold. The 80–20 rule is a heuristic that is employed to describe a wide range of phenomena. In the area of sales, it holds that 20 percent of our customers generate 80 percent of our business volume. In the quality arena, it suggests that 80 percent of our quality problems can be attributed to 20 percent of potential sources of problems.

In regard to competence, it can fairly be said that 20 percent of the employees of an organization contribute to 80 percent of the value created by the organization. That is, the success of an organization typically rests on the efforts of a small core of the workforce. Even political liberals have reluctantly come to acknowledge this fact. Robert Reich, a Harvard University professor, a professed political liberal, and secretary of labor in the first Clinton administration, states in his book *The Work of Nations* (1991) that about 20 percent of the U.S. population are *symbolic analysts,* the key individuals who drive the American economy. The remaining 80 percent are *in-service processors* and *routine production workers,* individuals whose added value to the economy is low.

The competence dilemma has created a situation that makes it difficult to address the issue of competence in an unemotional way. Although social and political perspectives may promote the view that people are equal, economics—the dismal science—suggests that people are different and will be rewarded for their efforts unequally.

What Is Project Management?

In a survey I conducted several years ago I asked more than a hundred project managers to define their jobs. These men and women responded with astonishing consistency. Roughly 80 percent of them said, "My job is to get the job done!" After some reflection, about half of them added, "The work must be done on time, within budget, and according to specifications." This caveat is heard so frequently that it has been given a name: the *triple constraint*. A moment's reflection suggests that all projects—whether they focus on building a space shuttle or simply entail cleaning the garage on a Saturday afternoon—operate under the constraints of time, budget, and specifications.

Clearly time is a crucial consideration in project management. After all, it is truly a nonrenewable resource—once it has passed, it can never be reconstructed. Beyond this, time has become a key competitive instrument. It is an axiom today that the faster an organization can turn around requests for action, the more competitive it is.

I experienced this phenomenon during a trip to Melbourne, Australia. I had come to Melbourne after spending a day shooting pictures at the spectacular Katoomba Falls in the Blue Mountains just two hours outside of Sydney. In Melbourne I looked for a place to process my three rolls of film. While walking down Elizabeth Street I came across three film-processing shops within two blocks. The first shop advertised that it could process pictures within twenty-four hours at an attractive, discounted price. The second advertised that it could process the pictures in an hour at a higher price. The third guaranteed that film processing would occur within half an hour at a still higher price. Given my impatience to see the results of my creative efforts, I will leave it to the reader's imagination to determine which shop received my business.

In project management, the time dimension is handled through scheduling. A variety of scheduling methodologies have been developed. The most commonly employed methodologies are Gantt charts, milestone charts, and PERT/CPM networks. A key element of determining the competencies of individuals in managing the time dimension is to assess their mastery of time-management scheduling techniques.

The second constraint of the triple constraints—budget—acknowledges that project work cannot be carried out without resources. We tend to view the budget constraint in monetary terms. For example, a project manager may find that she has been allocated $150,000 to implement a project to install a new computer system in a small company. It should be noted, however, that in the absence of monetary data, budgets can be construed as person-days of effort. That is, if I have five installers working fifteen days to install a piece of equipment, they consume a budget of seventy-five person-days of effort. If I know that the average wage expended on each installer is $150 per day, I can estimate that the dollar budget associated with this work is $11,250.

Currently many organizations (perhaps most organizations) have serious problems in tracking budget activity on their projects, because their accounting systems are based on general ledger accounting systems, which have little relevance to individuals attempting to track costs associated with the accomplishment of individual tasks. As companies increasingly direct their energies to organizing work as projects, they are adopting activity-based cost accounting systems that will enable them to track project costs.

In project management, the techniques employed to deal with the budget constraints include tools that allow for top-down and bottom-up cost estimates, capital budgeting techniques, life-cycle costing methodologies, and cost-control techniques. Competent project professionals should have some grasp of these cost-management techniques.

The third constraint—specifications—has undergone a radical transformation in how it is construed. Traditionally, the development of specifications was put into the hands of experts, who (it was presumed) knew best how to specify the requirements needed to produce a good. The problem with this approach is that solutions developed by experts might differ dramatically from solutions that address customers' true needs. Consequently, technically sound specifications might ultimately be rejected by customers, who fail to see the relevance of such specifications to the problems they face. Today the constraint of getting the job done according to specifications carries with it the significant caveat that the specifications must be established in such a way as to maximize customer satisfaction.

A distinguishing feature of project management is that it seeks to get the job done by using temporary, cross-functional teams. The temporary nature of these teams reflects the fact that projects are themselves temporary, one-shot undertakings. More often than not, the team members are borrowed resources—they come from functional areas, do their job, and then return to their functional homes. For example, during the design phase, design specialists may be brought in to do the design work. When they are done, implementers are brought in to build whatever is being developed. Periodically testers come on board to conduct tests. Toward the end of the project, operations and maintenance specialists may be hired to help with the cutover.

The temporary nature of projects, coupled with the heavy reliance on borrowed resources, presents project managers with major challenges. Generally managers have little direct control over the resources being employed. They do not "own" these resources because the resources are borrowed. Thus they often find themselves struggling to get who they need when they need them. Once the resources show up, project managers have problems motivating them, because managers have few carrots and sticks available as vehicles of motivation.

Project management has become a compelling management approach in these turbulent times for a number of reasons. For one thing, it is task focused and much of the work organizations carry out today is defined as tasks. Second, it enables organizations to tackle work using cross-functional teams, and today's complex problems require teamwork and often demand cross-functional solutions. Third, it is flexible and conducive to speedy solutions, because it makes use of borrowed resources (both internal and outsourced) as they are needed; this stands in marked contrast to what is encountered in rigid functional organizations, where the pool of resources is fixed. Finally, it epitomizes working through flattened structures (with their implications of worker empowerment) rather than the old hierarchies (which tend to support cumbersome top-down decision processes).

Conclusions

Intense global competition has forced individuals and organizations to change the way they do business. As more companies throughout the world have gained access to world-class technology, and as they have developed world-class management capabilities, they have begun to experience conditions associated with what economics textbooks call "perfect competition." When I studied microeconomics in the 1960s, my professor was careful to point out that perfect competition was chiefly a mental construct—it hardly existed in the real world. According to this professor, the only people who experienced something close to perfect competition were farmers, because they operated in a world of many producers, none of whom could individually have an impact on the market.

With the onset of the year 2000, near-perfect competition has become a reality in a wide array of industries. Buyers of goods and services are no longer limited to operating within the confines of their highly restricted local markets. In addition, because of advances in information technology, they are no longer hampered by imperfect information to guide them in their purchasing decisions. Thus, if a local supplier of goods and services does not meet their needs, they can take their business elsewhere—even to far-off lands whose geographic distance is increasingly irrelevant because of improvements in transportation and information technology.

This brave new world of near-perfect competition has had a tremendous impact on the workforce of men and women in all sectors of the global economy. In industrialized countries, global competition has shaken the underpinnings of the welfare state. Countries that pursued socially progressive policies—such as Germany, Sweden, and Canada—have found that they will have to cut back on their generous social programs or face bankruptcy. Medical benefits, unemployment allocations, and educational support stipends have been scrutinized carefully and cutbacks have been implemented.

The private sector has faced similar reassessments of its employment policies. Companies that have prided themselves on their generous employment policies have begun trimming their programs. For example, no companies that hope to compete effectively in world markets—markets that require using human and material assets flexibly—can offer their workers guarantees of lifetime employment.

Thus, as a consequence of the new economic forces at work in the world today, governments and businesses have radically altered the way they conduct their affairs. The litany of today's management hot buttons is well known and includes downsizing, outsourcing, flattened organizations, teamwork, continuous improvement processes, reengineering, and customer focus. Gone are the longstanding traditions of hierarchy, chains of command, job security, and worker loyalty.

To a large extent, the growing significance of project management as a management approach is rooted in the chaos associated with this messy world. Project management is comfortable in flattened organizations because it has always been based on the assembling of cross-functional teams. Project management lends itself to working with outsourced resources. Effective project leadership does not demand the existence of authority based on chains of command; rather, it recognizes that the best way to get the job done is through the effective use of influence.

But in a highly competitive world, project management by itself does not give individuals and organizations a competitive edge. Here is where the issue of competence emerges. To be a winner in today's competitive environment, individuals, teams, and organizations must operate as competently as possible in order to deliver goods and services faster, cheaper, and better than their competitors.

Chapter Two

Why Competence Pays

In the seventh chapter of Judges in the Hebrew Bible, Gideon is about to lead 32,000 Israelite troops into a battle against the Midianites. The Lord tells Gideon that he has too many troops and asks him to reduce the number. Gideon does this by informing the Israelites that anyone who is frightened of battle can leave the army. Twenty-two thousand men leave and 10,000 remain. The Lord then informs Gideon that the army is still too large. He suggests that Gideon observe how his men drink water from a pool. Those who get down on their hands and knees and drink water like dogs should be released from service. Those who use their hands to lift water up to their mouths should be retained. After applying this winnowing process, only 300 Israelites remain. The Lord now proclaims satisfaction with the size of the force, and using his rump army Gideon easily defeats the much larger forces of the Midianites. Like the U.S. Marines, Gideon finds that he can do the job most effectively with "a few good men."

Military commanders have long recognized that the quality of military forces is a key determinant of success. Consequently, over the millennia they have devised various rules of thumb for identifying competent performers. As the story of Gideon illustrates, sometimes the tests devised to measure competence are a bit idiosyncratic. I believe that most military services have abandoned Gideon's competency test! But even today, similarly idiosyncratic tests have not disappeared. As Jimmy Carter relates in his book *Why Not the Best?* (1975), Admiral Hyman Rickover would test the mettle of naval officers by interviewing them while they sat on a wobbly chair that had one leg purposely cut shorter than the other three. Rickover's intent in carrying out this exercise was to see how candidates for service in the nuclear navy functioned under adverse conditions.

Typically, the tests of competence are more conventional and based on the experience of what works and what does not. Consider Sun Tzu's list of "dangerous characteristics" of a general as described in his book, *The Art of War,* which was written 2,500 years ago. Sun Tzu based this list on experience. In his view, generals who possess the following five traits should be avoided: recklessness, cowardliness, quick temper, too much concern with honor, and compassion (1963, p. 115). When generals possess any of these traits, it can ruin their objectivity and harm their decision-making capabilities during crucial moments in battle. In Sun Tzu's words, "these five traits of character are serious faults in a general and in military operations are calamitous" (p. 115).

Competence is an issue because there are tremendous variations in people's abilities to do their jobs. If everyone possessed identical capabilities—that is, if we were wholly interchangeable, like parts of a machine—then searching for competent employees would become a nonissue. An employer could choose people at random and be assured of getting equal results. People do not possess equal capabilities, however. This becomes clear in the following simple illustration.

Let's assume that two people are given a task to carry out—say, to write a two-page description of corporate capabilities that will be employed in a sales brochure. One person may labor over this assignment for five days. He may spend two days gathering information on what the company has achieved over the past ten years. This may entail spending several hours interviewing colleagues to ascertain their viewpoints on corporate strengths. To make sure that he is on track, he may touch base with his manager four or five times a day to clarify points of which he is uncertain. In writing the material, he may struggle with the phrasing of each sentence. Again he may consult with colleagues and send them draft one, then draft two, and then draft three of his document in order to pick their brains.

The second person may be a wholly different animal. After receiving the assignment, she may take one morning to write a first-rate, two-page description of corporate capabilities. Not only does she do the job quickly, but unlike the first person she does not consume enormous amounts of her manager's and colleagues' time.

Anyone who works in the real world recognizes that this hypothetical example is not a caricature of people's capabilities; rather, it accurately portrays what happens. The truth is that the first person described in this example is more commonly encountered in organizations than the second. An additional truth is that the second person adds far more value to the organization's operations than the first.

One of the great project managers of modern times makes this point eloquently. Frederick Brooks was the project manager who developed the operating system for the IBM 360 computer in the mid-1960s. The IBM 360 propelled IBM to the position of being the leading contender in developing computers. Prior to the advent of the IBM 360, IBM was simply one of the pack, neither more powerful nor weaker than other contenders, such as Univac, Sperry, Remington Rand, and RCA. But after the IBM 360 mainframe computer entered the market, IBM became such a dominant player that it soon accounted for some 70 percent of world computer sales.

In his book *The Mythical Man-Month* (1975), Brooks notes that a key to the success of many of the projects at IBM was the employment of superprogrammers—people who could write ten times more high-quality code than the average programmer. The project team would be built around a superprogrammer, who Brooks labeled "the surgeon." Like a medical surgeon, the superprogrammer would have total control over his or her "operating theater." As with anesthesiologists, surgical assistants, and surgical nurses, the primary task of the project team members was to create an environment that enabled the surgeon (that is, the superprogrammer) to do his or her job effectively. Brooks clearly sees competent people as the key to project success and promotes the view that organizations should design project work around the efforts of the most competent players.

Variability in People's Ability to Do the Job

Dealing with the variability of people's capabilities can be quite controversial. A major source of controversy is that bigots use this kind of information to stereotype whole populations (such as Jews, Gypsies, and Slavs) in order to justify blatant racist policies against "inferior" races. In the United States, such controversies rage when respectable scholars (such as Jensen, 1969; Shockley, 1987; Herrnstein, 1971) dare to suggest that variations of some capabilities are genetically rooted. A controversy along these lines was generated with the publication of Richard J. Herrnstein and Charles Murray's book *The Bell Curve* (1994), which holds that a large portion of cognitive ability (a neutral term for intelligence) is hereditary and that highly intelligent people (as measured by IQ) generally do far better in life than individuals with lower levels of intelligence.

To my way of thinking, much of the controversy would be dissipated if people recognized that there are different types of competence and that within each type different levels of capability exist. In the IQ debate, Howard Gardner (1983) of Harvard University has taken precisely this approach, and I believe the perspective he offers makes much of the debate on intelligence irrelevant. Gardner proposes that there are in fact multiple intelligences. He specifically identifies seven:

- Musical intelligence
- Bodily-kinesthetic intelligence
- Logical-mathematical intelligence
- Linguistic intelligence
- Spatial intelligence
- Interpersonal intelligence
- Intrapersonal intelligence

A deficiency of IQ tests is that they tend to focus on only two of the seven intelligences: logical-mathematical and linguistic intelligence. I would add at least two more intelligences to Gardner's list. One would be "street smarts." I define this as the capacity to understand quickly the dynamics of a culture (in a nation, community, or organization) and then to operate in such a manner as to function effectively within it. (I often wonder how long many members of MENSA, an elitist society of people with high IQs, would survive in the streets of Hell's Kitchen in New York.)

A second intelligence I would add would be the intelligence associated with the capacity to think creatively. When I was a teenager,

I seriously considered becoming an artist. I recall reading a book that listed average IQ scores for different occupations and was mortified to find that painters—including Braque, Picasso, Rembrandt, and other notables—possessed IQs that were marginally higher than the average score of 100. I also noted that creative writers performed only a bit better than painters. Just recently I came across a newer study that listed average IQ scores by profession. At the top of the list—with scores higher than those for Ph.D. physicists—stood certified public accountants (CPAs)! To the naive this might suggest that Rembrandt was a dummy while Mortimer Snedley, CPA, is a genius. There is something terribly wrong with a system that could lead to such a conclusion. To me, the discrepancy between IQ scores and creative ability does not highlight deficiencies in the intellectual capabilities of creative people; rather, it suggests egregious deficiencies in what IQ tests attempt to measure.

Having said all this, I still maintain that there are obvious differences in people's abilities to do a job. This fact is so obvious that it does not merit debate. On a personal level, I know that I could take five years of piano lessons and at best hope to play "Chopsticks" competently at the end of my training. I have encountered an abundance of "professional" secretaries who after twenty years on the job are lucky to type thirty words per minute (even I, a "gifted amateur," routinely type sixty to seventy words per minute). I recently had a telephone installation technician visit my home who said he had worked for the telephone company for thirty years but who proved to be incapable of distinguishing hot wires from dormant wires. (It's a wonder he hadn't electrocuted himself yet!) He spent six hours doing a job that should have been accomplished in two. In view of the fact that the telephone company billed his time on an hourly basis, I did not appreciate being given an incompetent telephone installer.

The point is that there are obvious and dramatic differences in people's capabilities to carry out a job. Although these differences might have been glossed over in traditional bureaucratic organizations, today they can determine whether an organization stays in business and whether individuals keep their jobs.

Why were differences in people's abilities to do a job downplayed in traditional bureaucratic organizations? I can think of two basic answers to this question. First, a primary characteristic of bureaucracies is that they are governed by methods and procedures (that is, rules). A little thought shows that methods and procedures are designed to serve as substitutes for intelligence. With well-established methods and procedures, you do not need Albert Einsteins to run an organization. Average people can carry out complex tasks simply by learning the rules and following established methods and procedures for doing the work. In such an environment, there is no particular advantage to being more than marginally competent. The key competence is the capacity to understand and follow instructions.

Second, until quite recently there were more talented people than there were jobs that could employ them. The law of supply and demand was at work here, and because the supply of talent exceeded demand, there was not much advantage in possessing a high degree of competence. It has only been with the advent of advanced technologies in areas such as communications, computation, logistics, and transportation that the demand for people with basic competencies in areas such as mathematics, logical reasoning, software programming, operations research, design, and finance has exceeded the supply. One need merely read the classified advertisements in a big city newspaper to see this point. It is often noted that the greatest bottleneck to the advancement of information technology (IT) today is the shortage of qualified IT personnel in systems analysis, programming, testing, and software quality assurance.

The Primitive Economics of Competence

Today's focus on competence is driven largely by economics: the fact is, *it pays to be competent.*

This point is aptly shown in a simple illustration. John and Mary are house painters. They have been hired to paint two hundred identical rooms in a large building. They are each paid $100 a day for their work. After they begin their work, it becomes evident that Mary can paint a room twice as quickly as John. At the end of the first day, she has painted four rooms while John has painted only two. At the end of the second day, she has painted eight rooms while John has painted only four, and so on. An inspector examines the quality of their work and finds that there is no difference in the quality of their efforts—they both do an excellent job.

It should be evident that if John's and Mary's incomes reflect their abilities, a wage differential should exist: Mary should be paid more than John because she is able to achieve more work than he during a block of time. As things stand now, she makes $500 per week and paints twenty rooms in five days while John is also paid $500 per week but paints only ten rooms.

Let us assume that an industrial engineering study shows that John's output is average. He is neither better nor worse than the typical professional painter. This means that Mary is a superperformer, a highly competent worker. If John and Mary live in a free-market economy where labor is perfectly mobile and wages are determined by unfettered supply-and-demand forces in the labor market, Mary may start thinking about working for another employer who will demonstrate an appreciation of her productivity by paying her higher wages than John.

How much higher? The answer to this question depends on a number of factors. The easiest way to set Mary's wages would be to say that she should be paid twice as much as John because she produces twice as much work per unit of time. If John makes $500 a week to paint ten rooms, then Mary could ask for $1,000 a week to paint twenty. Looked at another way, with this scheme both are being paid $50 per room for their work.

Beyond this, in a society where quick work is highly valued, Mary might be paid a premium for her superproductivity. That is, she might be offered $1,100 per week. The logic here might be that slow work can lead to missed deadline dates, concomitant penalties, and loss of business—thus speedy work should be rewarded (in this case with a $100 bonus). Conversely, in a society where there is no perceived value in performing work quickly, Mary might find that her ability to negotiate a wage premium is limited.

The key feature distinguishing John and Mary's performance is speed. By restricting the illustration to only one distinguishing feature, the example was kept simple. In the real world, of course, things are not so simple. Although John may have painted rooms more slowly than Mary, he might also have produced higher quality work. Conversely, Mary's high energy level and good cheer might serve to motivate other painters in the company to do a better job. John, however, may possess good customer relations skills, a valuable asset when dealing with sensitive customers—and so on. Each worker brings a set of strengths and weaknesses that distinguishes him or her from the other workers and makes direct comparisons of abilities difficult.

The way to deal with this more complicated situation is to attempt to determine the amount of *value* added to the organization's operations by hiring either John or Mary. In economics this concept is called *value marginal product,* or VMP. The economic theory of wages holds that you should not pay workers more money than the value they add to the organization—their VMP.

To see this point, consider a simple example from the construction industry. Let's say that Mike Johnson is a project manager who has a long and distinguished track record of completing projects on time, within budget, and according to the specifications. Babel Tower Enterprises is reviewing Mike's resume and believes that he is the best qualified candidate to manage a major construction project to build a large office building. To win the construction project contract, Babel Tower Enterprises agreed to build the structure within a very short time frame. Any schedule delays would result in the company paying carrying charges, plus penalties of $10,000 per day.

A risk analysis shows that there is a high probability that the project will experience thirty working days of slippage unless the project team performs very well. That is, less-than-excellent performance may cost the company $300,000 in penalty expenses. If it is absolutely ensured that Mike can do the job on time, within budget, and according to specifications, and that an average project manager would experience thirty days of slippage, then *theoretically* Mike could be paid a premium of $299,999 and the company would still be one dollar richer by hiring Mike instead of an average project manager.

Why the Economics of Competence Dominates Today's World

The 1980s witnessed a major transformation of how organizations structure their activities. Traditional chain-of-command structures rapidly gave way to flatter structures. Bureaucratic decision processes waned while decentralized decision making waxed. Work that traditionally would be carried out in-house was increasingly contracted out. This transformation was not restricted to the economic realm. In the Soviet Union, for example, Mikhail Gorbachev launched a policy of *perestroika* (literally, "restructuring") to reformulate the Soviet political system.

The driving force behind this global transformation was competition. As the world evolved into a single marketplace, competition became intense. Local firms could no longer count on geography to provide them with competitive advantages in local markets. If they could not provide goods and services faster, cheaper, and better than the competition, their customers would take their business elsewhere—to the opposite side of the globe, if necessary.

Faster, cheaper, and *better* are the operating words of today's competitive environment. *Faster* indicates that today's customers require quick turnaround. They want their film processed in one hour, their jackets dry-cleaned in one hour, the oil changed in their automobiles in a half hour, their packages delivered anywhere in the country overnight. *Cheaper* means that they want goods and services delivered at the lowest price imaginable. Given easy access to pricing information, they often know very well what the prevailing price is and they will not pay a higher price. Finally, *better* suggests that they demand world-class quality. Companies that do not produce world-class goods and services have a difficult time staying in business.

Today's customers do not accept time, cost, and quality trade-offs. They reject statements like, "Sure, we can do the job more cheaply, but it will lead to a lower-quality deliverable" or "Yes, we can do the job faster, but it will cost you a lot more." They want it all, and if company A cannot deliver, company B will.

A little reflection will show that today's business environment supports providing high rewards to the high performers. Competence is what counts. For the first time in history, *what* you know is more important than *who* you know. This focus on competence is possible because of a number of economic realities that exist today.

First, as stated in Chapter One, many industries are experiencing conditions associated with what economics textbooks call *perfect competition.* This means that no one company can, through its actions, affect the price at which a good or service is offered. Perfect competition is the antithesis of *monopoly,* whose primary characteristic is that an individual firm can, through its actions, influence the price of a good or service. In today's near-perfect competition environment, businesses succeed because they are good and can produce goods and services faster, cheaper, and better than their competitors can.

Second, in many industries, customers have access to *near-perfect information.* They know what alternatives they face. For example, they know the price charged by different companies to provide a given good or service. They also know the detailed specifications of these individual offerings, so they can compare them across different vendors when they make purchasing decisions. For a firm to succeed in this environment, it has to provide customers with the best value. That is, it must produce the best products and services at the lowest prices, and do so in a timely fashion.

Third, today's labor markets are *open and flexible.* Workers dissatisfied with working conditions at one organization can try to sell their services to other organizations. In a lifetime employment environment, this is not possible, because mobility between organizations is viewed as betrayal and no one wants to hire a traitor. Open and flexible labor markets are a boon to the most competent workers, because such markets enable them to showcase their abilities and allow the marketplace to assign a value to them.

Taken together, these three contemporary economic realities create an environment in which the value of competent workers is appreciated and competence is highly rewarded.

The Growing Gap Between the High Performers and Everyone Else

As mentioned in Chapter One, in his book *The Work of Nations* (1991) Robert Reich identifies a category of workers who play a key role in their organizations and societies. He calls them *symbolic analysts,* because their distinguishing feature is that they manipulate concepts rather than physical things. They are the high performers, the people who make things happen. They include entrepreneurs, business leaders, scientists, engineers, artists, and writers. He points out that they possess three distinguishing characteristics: they are problem identifiers, problem solvers, and knowledge brokers. As problem identifiers, they have the good sense to devote their energy to addressing the real issues facing their organizations and not to be distracted by peripheral issues. As problem solvers, they produce results and enable their organizations to function effectively in a turbulent world. And as knowledge brokers, they know what is happening in the world at large, and in their industries in particular, and are well connected with other symbolic analysts.

Reich notes that today's world is evolving into a *meritocracy,* where people are rewarded according to their abilities. Although on the surface this fact may appear to be good, Reich points out that it has a dark side to it. That is, if people are rewarded according to merit, the gap between the haves and have-nots will widen, because capable people are a very scarce asset. Reich speculates that only 20 percent of the population qualifies as symbolic analysts, the movers and shakers of today's economy, and 80 percent do not; the latter fall into categories such as routine production workers (factory workers, for example) and in-process servers (such as employees at a fast-food restaurant). As demand for symbolic analysts grows, leading to elevated incomes, corresponding demand for routine production workers and in-process servers will decline.

To the extent that what Reich says is true—and statistical evidence in the United States suggests that the richest Americans are controlling a growing portion of national income—then the advent of a society in which rewards are based on merit will likely lead to social problems, as Reich predicts. He states that the key to keeping this from happening is to increase people's competence through education and training. When he became secretary of labor during the first Clinton administration, Reich practiced what he preached and became a significant advocate for educating and training disadvantaged segments of the American population.

A little reflection highlights an interesting fact: the people most threatened by a competence-based world order are not the poor—they already exist on the margins of society and have never enjoyed many of the benefits of a growing economy. Rather, most threatened are the great majority of the educated middle class, who by dint of their education and social position have automatically acquired high-paying jobs in the old bureaucratic organizations. One feature of bureaucratic organizations is that pay and performance are seldom directly linked. This is most evident in the case of middle managers, who are several levels removed from producing products and at the same time are several levels removed from providing the organization with the strategic direction it needs. In the 1980s, as organizations began rewarding people who most clearly added value to operations, they also began cutting loose people whose perceived value was nebulous—that is, middle managers.

Competence as a Sword and Shield

Today's turbulent business world is dominated by uncertainty. A company that is a business behemoth one day (such as Apple Computer, Xerox, Lotus, Digital Equipment, U.S. Steel, or Polaroid) may find itself struggling to survive the next day. What once would have been viewed as a great career coup (such as being appointed chief information officer [CIO] of a major corporation) is increasingly perceived as a kiss-of-death (CIOs today have an astonishingly high mortality rate). Today's hot product clutters the shelves of retailers tomorrow and can hardly be given away. It is a dynamic world. It is a dangerous world.

One great protector against this danger is competence. It is our sword and shield. Consumer tastes may vary from day to day, technology may change minute by minute, and the players with whom we must contend may fluctuate weekly; yet if individuals, teams, and organizations consistently deliver the goods on time, within budget, and according to the specifications, they can survive the chaos.

I constantly encounter the refrain from students and clients, "I have no authority, yet I have enormous responsibility. How can I win in such a situation?" My answer is, "Be the best you can be. If you are really good, people will listen. To be good, you must have the skills that enable you to add value to your organization's operations. In healthy organizations, no one will kill the goose that lays the golden egg. Your competence is your best defense."

Most of the discussion in this chapter has addressed the competence of individual people, but the idea of competence as a sword and shield applies to teams and organizations as well. For example, the high-performing team that consistently produces deliverables on time, within budget, and according to specifications is a *powerful* team. When the team members assemble to do a job, they catch management's attention. Everyone in the organization knows that they will achieve their goals. When team members say they need certain resources to do the job, no one doubts their assessment. Similarly, organizations that support their teams, possess consistent vision of what they should be doing, and produce first-class products and services are powerful and will prevail, even in turbulent times.

Conclusions

Competence pays because it leads to results, and as effective managers over the millennia—from Sun Tzu in China to Plato in Greece to St. Benedict in Rome to the governing board of the Dutch East India Company to Peter Drucker in more recent times—have noted, it is results that count. One of the more discouraging phenomena that managers encounter worldwide is the disappointment they feel when after a costly and extensive interviewing process they discover that the new people they just hired create more hassles than they resolve. Competent people, teams, and organizations do not increase hassles—they lessen them by producing intended results.

Chapter Three

Uncovering Organizational Pathologies

The premise of this book is that competence pays and that competent workers will receive their just rewards—provided that they work in environments that are not fettered with strong organizational pathologies. This is a rather strong proviso. Regrettably there is no shortage of organizational pathologies in business and government enterprises.

Organizations, like people, can display pathological behavior. This was the central theme of one of the best-selling humor books in the mid-1990s: *The Dilbert Principle* (Adams, 1996). The author reminds us that in the past, capable people were promoted within their organizations until they reached their level of incompetence—this is the basic postulate of the Peter Principle (Peter and Hull, 1969). In recent times, Adams points out, what he calls the Dilbert Principle (named after the central character of a cartoon series he created) has replaced the Peter Principle. That is, "The incompetent workers are promoted directly to management without ever passing through the temporary competence stage" (p. 12).

Organizational pathological behavior can be defined as behavior rooted in an organization's culture or procedures that works against the best interests of the organization and its members. Organizations in which messengers who bear bad news are punished demonstrate this pathology. Similarly, pathological behavior is displayed in organizations that persistently apply yesterday's solutions to today's problems, that focus only on the bottom line, whose management philosophy is driven by the *fad de jour,* and that engage in deception and corrupt business practices. Consequences of pathological behavior can include low profit margins, a profoundly unhappy workforce, disaffected customers, suboptimal operations, bankruptcy, and even the conduct of unethical and illegal activities.

Roots of Organizational Pathologies

The roots of organizational pathologies include contending stakeholder interests, decision makers who serve their personal interests at the expense of the organization's interests, dysfunctional cultures, pathological measurement and evaluation systems, clueless managers, lack of support for basic operations, corruption, and general incompetence. Each of these sources of organizational pathology is discussed briefly.

Contending Stakeholder Interests

One of the most perceptive treatments of decision making that I have encountered was written in the early 1970s by Graham Allison, a Harvard University professor. In his book *The Essence of Decision* (1971), Allison poses three different models that can be employed to interpret decision-making processes in organizations. In one perspective, he assumes that decision making is made by a rational actor. The *rational actor model* holds that in making a decision, people carefully weigh alternatives and ultimately choose the one that makes the most sense. A second perspective is the *operational procedures model*. In this case, decision making is driven primarily by following standard operating procedures (SOPs) established by the organization. If decision makers encounter one set of circumstances, the organization's SOP may suggest a particular course of action, whereas if they encounter a different set of circumstances, SOP will suggest a different course of action. For example, procedures might dictate that if a salesclerk encounters a customer with a complaint about a product, the issue should be directed automatically and immediately to the department manager. A third perspective is the *political model*. In this instance, different stakeholders struggle to have their desires prevail. They often see the decision-making process as a zero-sum game: one side wins at the expense of the other side. They devote enormous energy to resolving issues by means of political action. This may entail building coalitions with allies, taking preemptive steps to acquire resources before their opponents do, and undermining the position of their opponents. The political model is reminiscent of the principles preached by the social Darwinists in the nineteenth century: in their perspective, only the fittest survive.

Clearly the decision processes carried out in organizations contain elements of all three of Allison's decision-making models. To the extent that decisions are made objectively and are based on data that have been carefully gathered and analyzed, the organization follows a rational actor model. Decisions derived from market research studies are an example of this. These studies are carried out in an objective, rational fashion. Representative samples of customers are carefully chosen. Their purchasing preferences may be identified by means of carefully controlled investigations that often involve the analysis of questionnaire responses. Decisions are then made based on attentive consideration of the data. To the extent that decisions neatly dovetail with well-established organizational procedures, the organization follows the operational procedures decision-making model. Decisions to purchase goods and services typically fall into this category. For example, purchases of goods and services whose price lies above a predetermined threshold (say $25,000) may require competitive bidding from at least three vendors, while purchases of lower priced goods and services can bypass competitive bidding procedures. Finally, to the extent that decisions emerge from rough-and-tumble political processes, the organization is following the political model.

Effective decision making in organizations requires a balance in the employment of these three decision-making models. Organizational pathologies are evident when the balance is upset and the political model becomes the dominant mode of operation. When rational judgment becomes a secondary decision-making factor, when SOPs are willfully bypassed, and when the views of the winners of political struggles consistently prevail, then the organization is sick in some sense.

A fundamental problem encountered by organizations that operate in politically charged environments is that politically rooted solutions address issues that are of importance within the organization but that are often disconnected from external realities.

Organizational guerilla fighters who win victories over their opponents are often ill-equipped to deal with the outside world. In fact, their raze-the-crops strategies that are designed to damage their opponents may simultaneously weaken the organization. Ultimately, the victors of an internal political conflict may find themselves struggling in the external marketplace, where in an era of intense and open competition the real winners are organizations whose decisions are based on rationality and whose processes are most efficient—efficiencies gained by following SOPs!

Decision Makers Who Serve Their Personal Interests at the Expense of the Organization's Interests

There is nothing wrong with people pursuing their own interests. In fact, psychologists agree that people who work consistently against their own interests are the ones with problems. Masochists, for example, fall into this category.

The controlled pursuit of self-interest forms the basis of the free-market system. A little reflection shows that free markets are founded on the efforts of many buyers and sellers striving to maximize their profits. Players in the free market behave, quite frankly, selfishly. As long as markets are relatively competitive, this selfish behavior is salubrious and leads to vibrant economic activity. Selfish behavior becomes sinister, however, under conditions of monopoly. Monopolies lead to economic inefficiencies. Consumers pay more than needed for goods and services, and the quality of these goods and services tends to be inferior because there are no competitors pressing the monopolists to improve their offerings.

Organizational pathologies arise when decision makers make decisions primarily to serve their personal interests and when these personal interests are at variance with the organization's overall interests. Managers who implement policies not on the basis of merit but rather to gain the favor of higher level executives do not serve their organization's interests. By currying favor with superiors, they hope to advance their careers. They provide the feedback that they believe their superiors want to hear. Unfortunately, by taking such a stance they contribute to the isolation of upper management, whose decisions are based not on reality but on distorted information fed to them by sycophants.

Managers who use their control over resources to strengthen their power within the organization also contribute to organizational pathology. They see these resources as part of their personal treasure trove and dispense them like monarchs granting favors to loyal subjects. Similarly, they withhold resources from people they view as disobedient, disloyal, or threats to their power.

Managers who make personnel decisions to reward friends and punish enemies help destroy the moral fabric of the organization and create tremendous morale problems among the workforce. This phenomenon is particularly destructive when it is the highest level of management that abuses the personnel system. The CEO who develops a pattern of nurturing successors then dismissing them when they display strength, only to replace them with new successors who in turn will be dismissed, is a phenomenon that is common among autocratic senior executives who are reluctant to relinquish their power. The employees of the organization are not blind to this type of pathological behavior and the most competent among them will be reluctant to serve in leadership positions that will lead to their demise.

What I have offered here is a short list of pathological behavior rooted in managers' excessive pursuit of self-interest. The antithesis of grossly selfish managers are altruistic managers. Happily, my sense is that in effective organizations altruistic managers are the rule rather than the exception. In a healthy organization, grossly selfish managers are easily spotted and find that their pathological behavior is unacceptable.

Dysfunctional Organizational Cultures

Organizational pathology may be rooted in an organization's adherence to a dysfunctional culture. Dysfunctional cultures can be viewed from several different perspectives. I focus on only two cases here: cultures that are excessively ideological and cultures that lack solid values.

Examples of excessive ideology abound in the business world. A company preoccupied with maintaining a revenue growth rate of 20 percent per year at any price is asking for trouble, as is a company whose every action must contribute to its building of innovative capabilities. Companies that liken themselves to Navy Seal units, that consider employees who work fewer than sixty hours per week to be laggards, and that view employees who discuss their salaries with other employees as disloyal similarly possess ideologically rooted cultural pathologies.

A common ideologically rooted pathology is something I call *macho management.* This pathology is well illustrated in Tracy Kidder's book *The Soul of a New Machine* (1981). This book describes Data General's attempt to build a minicomputer that would enable it to compete against Digital Equipment's market-dominating VAX computers. The corporate culture in which project team members found themselves oozed testosterone. Team members visualized themselves as gunslingers. They lived by the credo, "Ours is not to reason why, ours is but to do or die." In the end, Data General's young and talented engineers were able to produce a competent minicomputer in record-breaking time. Conversely, at the end of the project the majority of these engineers left the company. Kidder's assessment suggests that most of them felt unfulfilled by their experience, and this feeling appeared to be tied to the cold, uncaring, macho environment in which they functioned.

The opposite of an organization that possesses excessive ideology is one that lacks values. I suspect that more organizations fit into this category than into the ideological category. In these organizations, employees have little sense of what the organization is about. They operate in a passionless environment. They do not understand where the organization is headed and where it is coming from. They sense that the organization is spiritually adrift.

To deal with this problem, in the late 1980s and early 1990s thousands of organizations undertook exercises to identify their visions and define their missions. Unfortunately, in many cases their employees correctly surmised that these vision-and-mission exercises were chiefly pro forma and did not reflect a real commitment by the management of their organizations to identify the organization's values. In fact, many workers viewed vision-and-mission exercises through prisms of cynicism, noting that even as task forces were creating noble statements of purpose, large numbers of workers were losing their jobs.

Poor Measurement and Evaluation Procedures

In the 1990s, organizations began adopting Lord Kelvin's dictum, stated in the nineteenth century, that if one cannot measure a phenomenon, then one's conclusions about it are weak and speculative. Management specialists recognize that what applies in physics—Lord Kelvin was one of the great physicists of his time—might be transferable to the realm of management. That is, management decisions based on measurable facts are generally stronger than decisions based on unsupported gut feeling.

Many organizations have sought to implement measurement systems to enable them to make more rational business decisions. Although the motivation to base decision making on measurable behavior is noble, when applied naively it contributes to organizational pathology. This is amply illustrated in the following real-world examples.

Commissions paid to salespeople based on revenues generated. Anyone who has worked in an organization that rewards its sales staff by paying them commissions on revenues generated recognizes that such a system can lead to pathological behavior. The roots of the pathology lie in the fact that if an organization possesses reasonably attractive goods and services, it is quite easy to increase revenues *by lowering price.* Of course, if the price is low enough, goods and services are being offered below costs and the organization is losing money. So even as the sales staff are earning handsome commissions for generating business, the company might be inching its way toward bankruptcy.

Revenues are also easy to generate if the sales staff promise customers that the organization can deliver products and services more quickly than is physically possible, or that it can add features that the engineers cannot actually deliver. Thus a company may gain business based on promises that cannot be kept. This of course leads to profound customer unhappiness and, ultimately, to the loss of business.

Performance appraisals based on meeting quotas in the shipment of goods. Project team members in one large computer company I worked with complained that a predicament they faced was that the equipment their company produced was consistently being shipped to customers earlier than promised. This was a problem because the customers were not prepared to receive the equipment at the early dates (for example, they might not have facilities to store the equipment). Consequently, they would reject the shipments.

It turned out that the root of the problem was that salespeople faced quarterly quotas in which a certain threshold volume of equipment would have to be shipped each quarter. As the quarter drew to a close and it became apparent that the quotas would not be fulfilled, the sales staff would request that the manufacturing department ship equipment earlier than planned. In this way they would meet their quotas. Unfortunately, the early shipments disrupted project plans and irritated customers.

Performance appraisals based on use of materials consumed. Back in the days of central planning in the Soviet Union, the manager of a tableware manufacturing plant was ordered to double production of plates, cups, and saucers. The manager knew that auditors would determine his compliance with the directives by tracking the amount of clay his plant consumed. He also knew that the directives were unrealistic, because he was given no new equipment to increase his output. To demonstrate his compliance with the directives, he consumed twice the volume of clay that went into the making of the tableware. He did this, however, by making each plate, cup, and saucer heavier—not by producing more items.

Bonuses based on the speed of customer transactions. As organizations conduct more and more business over the telephone, a major issue they must deal with is that their employees may linger during the calls in order to chat with clients. One company I worked with tried to promote efficiency in processing customer phone transactions by providing a bonus each quarter to the employee who processed the largest number of transactions. The employee who won the first bonus beat out other employees by an astonishing margin. When she won the second bonus with an even larger margin of victory, a suspicious manager investigated the key to her success. It turned out that whenever she received a phone call from a person with a foreign accent, she would hang up on that person because she realized that it would take longer to communicate with an individual whose mastery of English was imperfect. This strategy enabled her to win efficiency bonuses—but no doubt it led to customer unhappiness and the loss of business.

Bonuses to fix bugs. In *The Dilbert Principle,* Scott Adams (1996) relates a story in which a manager offered to pay quality assurance staff $20 for each bug they found and his programming staff $20 bonuses for each bug they fixed. Clearly this bonus system was not well conceived, because the people who were receiving rewards for debugging were the same people who had created the bugs in the first place. The bonus plan was put on hold when in the first week one programmer netted $1,700.

Clueless Managers

One of the more demoralizing experiences employees encounter in their careers is working for clueless managers. These are men and women who are oblivious to the impacts of their words and actions. Their attempts at humor are offensive. They provide little feedback about the job performance of their workers, and when feedback is forthcoming it may entail ad hominem attacks on the employees. Frequently the images these managers have of their roles are shaped by having viewed too many movies portraying Hollywood's vision of the business environment. That is, they wear the mantle of captains of industry and issue orders like generals running a military campaign. Regrettably these orders often have not been thought through and lead to predictably unfortunate consequences.

The phenomenon of clueless managers can reach up into the highest levels of the organization. In the early 1990s, *Business Week* featured an article titled "CEO Disease" (Byrne, Symonds, and Siler, 1991), which addressed the question, Why are organizations that possess an abundance of energetic and talented younger managers headed by CEOs who are so out of touch with reality? One conclusion: top management surrounds itself with a bevy of men and women who are adept at telling management whatever they want to hear. In turn, the men and women who provide their bosses with the information they want to hear find themselves rewarded for their cooperative behavior. The pathological nature of this behavior is evident.

In his book *Emotional Intelligence*, psychologist Daniel Goleman (1995) suggests that clueless managers lack a number of basic traits. First, they lack empathy skills. Empathy is the ability to put oneself into the shoes of other people. When people lack empathy skills— that is, when they are unable to feel what other people are experiencing—they cannot be effective in dealing with those people. In a related vein, clueless managers have weak interpersonal skills. They are awkward in dealing with people. They talk too long, tell tasteless jokes, and are unable to read nonverbal cues emanating from the people with whom they are dealing (this last condition is called *dyssemia,* from the Greek *dys,* difficulty, and *semes,* signal). Finally, clueless managers lack what Howard Gardner (1983) calls intrapersonal skills. That is, they do not have a good grasp of themselves—of their own desires, needs, and capabilities. It is difficult to see how people who do not understand themselves can be expected to understand and deal effectively with others.

Lack of Support for Basic Operations

I was once asked by the top management of an engineering company in the telecommunications industry to help the organization design a project management structure that would enable it to carry out its projects more effectively. After interviewing some thirty managers and project workers over a period of two days, it became evident that the key challenge facing the company was not the structuring of its project efforts. Rather, the principal challenge was to discard its old order-processing systems (it had three systems functioning and none was linked to the others) and replace them with a fully integrated system. As things stood, once a customer signed up to receive project services from this company, it became virtually impossible to track the progress of the order. Without an effective order-processing system, account executives could not answer customer inquiries and project management procedures could not be implemented.

Similarly, the greatest impediment to effective cost control on projects is the lack of activity-based accounting systems. In a study I conducted a few years ago, only 30 percent of the project workers I surveyed reported having usable cost data on their projects. A major source of problems was that their companies' accounting systems were general ledger systems and these did not provide useful cost data at the level of individual tasks. Consequently, the project workers were unable to determine the cost status of their efforts. Many of these people echoed the sentiment of one survey respondent who said to me, "Frankly, on my projects I don't have any idea as to whether I am making or losing money."

Lack of support to carry out basic operations can take many additional forms. Workers who have access only to obsolete equipment are hampered from doing the best job possible. Staff who do not receive training on how to use newly introduced technology cannot function effectively. A physical work environment that is depressing will not spur workers to higher levels of productivity.

Corruption and Greed

Perhaps the most obvious example of an organization experiencing a pathological situation is one that is riddled with corruption and driven by greed. Names like Michael Milken, Ivan Boesky, Dennis Levine, Robert Maxwell, and Barry Minkow conjure up images of organizations whose operations were founded on lies. Books like *Barbarians at the Gate* (Burrough, 1990) suggest that even when outright criminal behavior does not exist, outrageous greed can serve as the basis of pathological behavior.

While levels of corruption in the industrialized countries are disappointingly high, they are astronomical in some of the world's fastest growing economies, such as China, Taiwan, Korea, Thailand, India, Indonesia, Mexico, and Brazil. Men and women slated to work in corruption-filled societies had better prepare themselves to deal with the seamier sides of business.

General Incompetence

Clearly, organizational pathology exists when an organization's members display general incompetence. In recent years I accurately predicted the demise of a hardware store chain, a fast-food restaurant chain, and a hotel simply by noting the astonishing level of incompetence reflected in their day-to-day operations. What was clear was the pervasiveness of incompetence in all aspects of the organizations' activities. For example, in each of these organizations, service provided by employees was sloppy. In the hardware store, items were marked with the wrong prices, and it took an eternity to pay for goods at the checkout counter. In the fast-food restaurant, customer lines grew intolerably long while employees frolicked in the kitchen. In addition, tables were dirty and trash lay on the floor. In the hotel, it took nearly two hours to order a simple meal, and when the food arrived it was inedible. Room service seldom came to pick up dinner trays. At checkout, customers were commonly served with a bill for another person's room. It was no surprise when each of these organizations went out of business.

General incompetence is rooted in a plethora of factors. For example, employees from the top to the bottom may lack the basic skills and will to do their jobs effectively. The organization may lack effective procedures to carry out its operations. When it does have sound procedures, it may lack the discipline to enforce them. The organization's culture may be ill defined. The organization may not provide the right kinds of support—information systems, technology, clerical help—to enable its employees to operate effectively in a highly competitive environment.

Conclusions

Competence cannot be nurtured in sick organizations. Just as the sprinter who suffers from influenza cannot be expected to run a good race, competent performance will not be found in unhealthy organizations. One thing is increasingly certain in today's world, where the most competent workers are in high demand and short supply: the very best performers will not stick around the sick organization. They will move on to more fertile fields, because they recognize that their capabilities cannot flourish in dysfunctional environments. Why should they put up with nonsense in a sick organization when they can blossom in a healthy one?

The implications of this reality are clear: organizations suffering from some of the pathologies described in this chapter cannot expect to excel. Hiring supercompetent performers at astronomical salaries will not help as long as underlying pathologies exist. As the old saying goes, you can't make a silk purse out of a sow's ear. For these organizations to achieve competence, they must first recognize the pathologies from which they suffer. They must then take steps to remedy them. Only then can they seriously consider what steps should be taken to achieve high levels of competence.

Part Two

The Competent Project Professional

Chapter Four

The Project Professional's Knowledge Base

One of the key traits of some of America's most enduring television comedians is their fundamental incompetence. In the 1950s, in *I Love Lucy*, Lucille Ball played a well-intentioned bumbler whose basic ineptitude was constantly getting her in trouble. Her television contemporary Ralph Cramden of *The Honeymooners* (played by Jackie Gleason) was a self-important know-it-all who, when the bombast was stripped away, was clearly an incompetent. He was constantly dreaming and scheming and, like Lucy, creating enormous problems for himself. Both Lucy and Ralph were fortunate, however, because despite their ineptitude, things always worked out well for them by the end of the TV program.

In the 1980s and 1990s, the incompetence of the key players continued to be a theme of TV comedy, but their incompetence assumed a somewhat sinister flavor. This is evident in such big comedic hits as *Married with Children, Roseanne,* and *The Simpsons*. There is little endearing about the lead characters in these programs (Al Bundy, Roseanne Connor, and Homer Simpson, respectively). Each of them heads a dysfunctional family. They are losers who build their self-esteem by mocking traditional virtues such as honesty, hard work, and competence.

Why are TV programs that focus on incompetent characters so popular? To me the answer is simple: the laughter we hear when Al Bundy is shown winning a contest by cheating a capable adversary is a *nervous* laughter rooted in the insecurities of the viewing audience. They identify with Al Bundy, not with his capable adversary. On TV, Al Bundy can beat his better-qualified adversary by subterfuge and dissimulation, but everyone knows that in the real world the capable adversary will eat Al Bundy for breakfast.

A primary goal of the effective worker should be to emulate Bundy's competent adversary, not Bundy. In the real world, the skilled, well-prepared individual consistently outperforms the confused laggard. With the decline of bureaucracy and labor unions, people in the work world are being held accountable for their performance. They can no longer camouflage themselves in the bureaucracy's labyrinth or protect themselves with union work rules. If they want to earn a good living and possess some measure of job security, they must demonstrate their basic competence.

The Competent Project Manager

In the mid-1990s, I carried out a focus-group exercise with several hundred men and women who were experienced project professionals. I asked them to describe to me what they perceived to be the desirable traits of a competent project manager. The initial list that emerged from this process was quite long. I worked with the focus group members to consolidate the traits, and what finally emerged are the following items. The order in which the items appear is random and is not intended to suggest priorities.

The competent project manager should do the following:

• *Be a results-oriented, can-do individual.* Carrying out projects is about achieving results. Project success and failure are largely determined by identifying the degree to which the desired results have been attained. Effective project professionals are obsessed with achieving results and they do not allow distractions to draw their attention away from their defined goals.

• *Have a head for details.* Project professionals are inundated with facts and figures—budgets, deadlines, technical specs, promises made—and must avoid being overwhelmed by them. While they must always keep an eye on results and assume a big-picture perspective on the project, they must simultaneously "sweat the details."

• *Possess a strong commitment to the project.* The word *commitment* has several implications. It is closely associated with a number of concepts, including dedication, ownership, and follow-through. Committed project workers are men and women who are willing to do what it takes to get the job done. Quite often this translates into spending substantial amounts of time working on the project. Project managers who work forty-hour weeks are rare birds.

• *Be aware of the organization's goals.* For project managers to operate effectively, they should be fully familiar with their organization's goals and be committed to achieving them. They should make sure that in implementing their projects they serve these goals and convey their content to project team members.

• *Be politically savvy.* One of the basic realities of project management is that typical project managers have little direct control over the resources employed on their projects, because the resources are chiefly borrowed. They cannot achieve results by *commanding* outcomes. Rather, they achieve them through *influence.* Politics is the art of influence. The implication of this basic project reality is clear: to do their jobs effectively, project managers need to develop political skills.

• *Be cost conscious.* A fundamental requirement for organizational success today is cost consciousness. For organizations to be competitive they must deliver their goods and services at the lowest possible prices. In the 1990s, the reengineering movement accelerated the drive to reduce costs because it preached that most organizations could dramatically increase their profitability by streamlining their business processes. In carrying out their work, project managers should be sensitive to costs and should strive to implement their projects in a cost-effective manner.

• *Understand business basics.* Although cost consciousness is important, it is not enough. One can be frugal but still lack good business sense. Effective project managers should possess a firm grasp of a wide range of knowledge-based business skills in the areas of planning, control, marketing, operations, and financial management. Beyond this, they should possess good business judgment and the capacity to make decisions that will enhance the performance of their operations. (The need for solid business competencies is discussed in detail in Chapter Seven.)

• *Be capable of understanding the needs of staff, customers, and management.* Project managers spend most of their time dealing with people (project staff, management, customers, and vendors). In order to deal with these people effectively, project managers must possess good empathy capabilities. That is, they must be able to put themselves into the shoes of other people in order to see the world from a different perspective. Project managers who are insensitive to the needs and wants of their staff, customers, and management will certainly face an abundance of people problems. (The need for "emotional intelligence" in project managers is discussed in detail in Chapter Six.)

• *Be capable of coping with ambiguity, setbacks, and disappointments.* Little is clear in these turbulent times. This is particularly true in the project environment, because project managers do not possess many carrots and sticks, chains of command are absent, work is often carried out by contractors, and requirements are constantly changing. In such an environment, project managers find that it is not easy to have their will prevail. Consequently they encounter many setbacks. It is important that they not be easily discouraged.

• *Possess good negotiation skills.* On typical projects, different stakeholders work actively to promote their interests and these interests are frequently divergent. Project managers often find themselves in situations where key stakeholders do not support their efforts. In these situations, it is important for project managers to be able to negotiate workable solutions to the conflicts they encounter. This means that they cannot be stubborn and they should not view decision making as a win-lose proposition. Effective negotiation requires that negotiators strive for win-win solutions to problems.

• *Possess the appropriate technical skills to do his or her job.* If project managers operate in the accounting profession, they should have solid accountancy skills. If they are bridge builders, they should have good civil engineering skills. The possession of appropriate technical skills is necessary if project managers are to be viewed as credible leaders by their project teams.

When I showed a list of these items to a group of project professionals, one blurted out, "The only trait missing from the list is 'walk on water.'" This comment is quite insightful. We expect a great deal of our project managers. I sometimes quip that we do not expect our CEOs to possess even half the capabilities that we demand of effective project managers.

Of course no one individual scores perfectly on each of the items in the list of desirable traits. We each have our strengths and weaknesses. It is evident, however, that the stronger an individual is across the range of the listed traits, the more effective he or she will be as a project manager.

People who are strong on a large number of the listed traits possess value that is reflected in the salaries being paid to project managers. A survey I conducted in 1995 of fifteen major project-focused organizations suggests that experienced project managers are well compensated. Within these fifteen organizations, the salary level for senior project managers ranged from a low of $90,000 per year to a high of $220,000. The salary range for midlevel project managers went from a low of $55,000 to a high of $85,000, with a typical salary of about $65,000. For entry-level project managers, salaries ranged from $45,000 to $65,000, with a typical salary of $55,000. Considering that the average 1995 salary of U.S. managers in general stood at $45,000 per year, the compensation provided to project managers appears generous indeed.

To show that the link between the desired traits and income is not an abstraction, consider the following job placement advertisement appearing in the London *Times* on June 18, 1998 (p. 30):

Project Managers

Package to 100,000 pounds per annum [that is, $160,000 in U.S. dollars]. Our client is looking for two IT professionals to undertake critical development roles. . . . What are we looking for? Solid career track record . . . project management, business analysis and/or consultancy experience; familiarity with managing and motivating technical personnel; ability to work successfully with a wide range of talents, experience and knowledge; and a sense of purpose and spirit which sets new standards for Getting the Job Done.

Note that the description of desired traits contained in this ad focuses less on technical capability and more on business and management competence. The employer is looking for someone who can produce results, not for an expert on PERT/CPM scheduling.

Attempts to assess the competence of individuals should be broken into three parts. One part should examine knowledge-based competencies. The second part should review what I call socially rooted competencies. Finally, the third part should address good business judgment. This chapter and the next focus on knowledge-based competencies, and Chapters Six and Seven examine socially rooted and good business judgment competencies.

Knowledge-based competencies are the objective knowledge that individuals are expected to possess in order to carry out their jobs effectively. A C++ software language programmer should know something about programming in C++, just as a mason should know something about working with stone and concrete and a surveyor should know something about using a theodolite.

Socially rooted competencies are more subjective. They focus on abilities such as good judgment and human relations skills. Task leaders who are able to mediate conflicts on their teams possess some measure of socially rooted competence, as do project managers who can motivate borrowed resources to put in needed extra hours of work, and technical workers who display sensitivity to their customers' needs.

Business-judgment competencies are tied to the ability of individuals to make decisions that consistently serve the best business interests of the organization. People who are strong in this area are able to assess the risks and rewards associated with decisions they are about to make. They look beyond the immediate impact of their decisions and understand their opportunity costs. Although they recognize the importance of establishing and following good methods and procedures for the effective functioning of the organization, they do not behave like mindless bureaucrats. When they see an opportunity to improve business performance, they seize it, even when it lies outside the realm of defined procedures.

Assessing Knowledge-Based Competence

Determining an individual's level of knowledge-based competence is relatively straightforward because it can be tested. If it is determined that being able to calculate the mean value of a list of numbers is an important competence for a bookkeeper to possess, potential bookkeepers can be given a string of numbers and asked to compute their average value. If schedulers should be able to determine the critical path of a schedule, they can be given some basic schedule data and asked to compute its critical path. If contract managers should be able to distinguish the differences between cost-plus-award-fee and cost-plus-incentive-fee contracts, they can be asked questions requiring them to highlight the differences between these two contract mechanisms. Through simple testing it is possible to develop a sense of an individual's mastery of knowledge-based competence.

Organizations have been involved in measuring knowledge-based competence for a long time. For example, it is common practice to administer a test to applicants for a technical job that requires them to demonstrate their mastery of the required skills. Aspiring civil engineers might be required to calculate the load that a beam of given dimensions and given material can bear. A potential Pascal software programmer may be asked to write a number of software routines in Pascal. An applicant for a job at a tax-preparation firm may need to recite the implications associated with recent changes in the tax code.

The knowledge-based competencies of existing employees are also commonly reviewed. When functional managers write annual performance appraisal reviews for their staff, questions they typically address include, Does the employee know his or her business well? Has he or she kept up with the latest developments in the field? In some measure, the assessment of knowledge-based competence is embedded in management by objectives, or MBO (Drucker, 1954). An important part of the MBO process is to determine whether employees have achieved their defined goals on time. Presumably their ability to achieve these goals consistently reflects, to some degree, their level of competence.

Assessment of project management knowledge-based competence is not new. Organizations in traditional project-focused industries, such as the construction and defense industries, have long made mastery of project management skills a prerequisite for assuming major project responsibilities. More recently, even organizations new to project management have set up formal procedures for assessing these competencies. For example, in the late 1980s AT&T and Computer Science Corporation took steps to create internal project management certification programs. In the early 1990s IBM launched such a program that has been implemented quite successfully. Hughes Aircraft and Fannie Mae have also created project management tracks in their programs to certify the management capabilities of their employees.

Although these various attempts at measuring project management competence have been admirable efforts, they have suffered from a number of deficiencies. The chief deficiency is that these competency measuring efforts have been excessively parochial. They have tended to focus on the internal conditions of the organization of immediate interest to management. For example, one organization I encountered initially defined project management competence as the capacity of an employee to master the 128 steps needed to install a certain class of telecommunications equipment at client sites. Another deficiency was that the employees found little satisfaction in jumping through the competency hoops set up for them by management. Many of them spent enormous amounts of time preparing for the competency assessments and then after achieving certification their reaction was, "So what? No one recognizes my achievement outside of the narrow confines of my organization."

Individuals and organizations have begun to see that what is needed is an internationally recognized approach to assessing the project management competencies of project workers. This approach should go beyond addressing the parochial interests of individual organizations. It should be based on a well-established body of knowledge. It should in fact give rise to the feeling that project management has become a profession, just as medicine, law, accounting, and engineering are viewed as professions. The creation of the Project Management Institute's (PMI) certification examination in 1984 was an attempt to fill this need.

The certification examination developed by PMI was designed to measure the knowledge-based competencies of project professionals. PMI identified eight basic functional competencies that project professionals should master, as well as a ninth competency that demands the ability to integrate project efforts. The eight functional competencies are as follows:

1. *Scope management.* Scope management takes a big-picture view of projects. It is concerned with such broad issues as developing scope statements, constructing work breakdown structures, understanding what happens in the different stages of the project's life cycle, selecting projects, establishing project charters, and managing changes to project requirements using techniques such as configuration management.

2. *Time management.* Time management is the one competency that the project management discipline "owns," because project

THE PROJECT PROFESSIONAL'S KNOWLEDGE BASE

management's most unique skills revolve around scheduling project efforts. Key time management techniques that capable project professionals should be able to use include Gantt charts, milestone charts, and PERT/CPM charts. Tracking schedule performance using the earned value technique is another important competence that effective project professionals should master.

3. *Cost management.* Cost management focuses on cost estimating (both the bottom-up and top-down varieties), basic budgeting, life-cycle costing, principles of business economics, capital budgeting, and cost control using the earned value technique.

4. *Human resource management.* Human resource management covers a substantial amount of territory. In the project management arena, the chief human resource management concerns are directed at managing conflict, motivating borrowed resources, managing in a matrix environment, building authority, coping with project politics, and employing resource allocation tools such as the responsibility matrix, the resource Gantt chart, and the resource loading chart.

5. *Risk management.* Risk management is concerned with decision making under conditions of imperfect information. Project managers who are competent in managing risk should understand how to identify risks, how to determine their impact (such as through scenario building, modeling, or Monte Carlo simulation), and how to mitigate them (such as through risk deflection, risk avoidance, and the establishment of contingency reserves). A basic grasp of risk management requires an elementary understanding of statistics, including the concepts of expected value and statistical distributions, and the employment of decision trees.

6. *Quality management.* Quality management is directed at producing goods and services that maximize customer satisfaction. Effective quality management requires that project staff be sensitive to customers' needs and wants. Quality management principles and techniques that project professionals should grasp include quality control (such as use of control charts), the zero defects concept, distinguishing random from assignable variances, use of Pareto diagrams to identify the major sources of quality problems, and approaches to sampling.

7. *Procurement management.* The procurement management competency is concerned with basic issues of outsourcing project

work as well as with purchasing issues. Competent project professionals should have some understanding of the principles associated with different contract mechanisms, such as firm-fixed-price contracts, cost-plus-fixed-fee contracts, cost-plus-award-fee contracts, cost-plus-incentive-fee contracts, and time-and-materials contracts. In addition, they should have broad knowledge of the functions of requests for proposals (RFPs) and statements of work (SOWs). They should appreciate the role of negotiations in developing contracts and should know how to deal with possible sources of conflict on contracts.

8. *Communication management.* The communication management competency is the "softest" of the eight project management competencies discussed here. That is, there are few clearly defined techniques and principles associated with this competency. This is not to say that it is an unimportant matter, because good communication lies at the heart of effective project management. Basic topics associated with this competency include an understanding of the communication model (that is, the roles of sender, receiver, encoding, decoding, the medium, and feedback), an appreciation of the strengths and weaknesses of different approaches to communication (such as verbal versus nonverbal), and the functions of different kinds of meetings (such as kickoff meetings, status reviews, informal get-togethers, technical reviews, and crisis meetings).

In addition to these eight competencies, PMI has identified a ninth "metacompetence" called *integration management.* As its name implies, this competence is the ability of individuals to integrate the eight somewhat disparate competencies just described. PMI has developed a full treatment of these competencies in a document titled *Guide to the Project Management Body of Knowledge (PMBOK)* (Duncan, 1996).

Checklist of Tools

It is certainly possible that people can run projects effectively without mastering the intricacies of many of the well-known project management tools. One can argue convincingly that one of the most effective contemporary masters of complex projects is movie director Steven Spielberg, who in a large number of movie productions (including *Jaws, Close Encounters of the Third Kind, ET,* the

Indiana Jones movies, *Jurassic Park, Schindler's List,* and *Saving Private Ryan*) consistently got the job done on time, within budget, and according to specs. Despite Spielberg's obvious competence in carrying out projects, it would be surprising to learn that he could define a critical path or construct a work breakdown structure. Of course *someone* in Spielberg's operation (most likely a *team* of people) has mastered scheduling, budgeting, and resource allocation techniques. Otherwise, Spielberg's movies simply could not be produced cost-effectively.

Each profession has its tools, and mastery of the tools is one of the key goals of the professional. This section offers an abbreviated list of the key tools associated with each of the eight PMBOK functional areas. This list should be viewed as a simple checklist. As you go over the list, ask yourself, Am I conversant with this tool? Can I actually employ it? If in considering these questions it becomes apparent that you have some knowledge gaps, think about filling those gaps through coursework or self-study.

Scope Management Tools

Work breakdown structure: A product-oriented listing of key elements of the project

Benefit-cost analysis: A project selection tool that requires organizations to assess the relative benefits of a proposed project and contrast these with project costs

Configuration management: A change-control methodology that requires meticulous documentation of changes to the project

Time Management Tools

Gantt chart: A bar chart that portrays simply how different tasks are laid out over time

Milestone chart: A chart that pictures key milestones against a time line

PERT/CPM chart: A network diagram that shows the dependency relationships of tasks

Earned-value technique: A cost-accounting methodology that allows analysts to perform integrated cost-and-schedule-control reviews of projects

Cost Management Tools

Cost-estimating techniques: Top-down and bottom-up techniques employed to estimate project costs

Cumulative cost curve: A method that enables staff to compare actual versus planned costs over time in order to identify levels of cost variances (also called the S-curve)

Life-cycle costing: An overview of project costs that looks at operations and maintenance costs in addition to project costs

Capital budgeting tools: Basic financial investment techniques, including present-value analysis, internal rate of return, and pay-back-period analysis

Earned-value technique: A cost-accounting methodology that allows analysts to perform integrated cost-and-schedule-control reviews of projects

Human Resource Management Tools

Motivation and team-building techniques: Techniques that focus on motivating matrixed resources

Management by objectives: A management approach that requires the creation of unambiguous and achievable objectives

Responsibility matrix: A simple chart that juxtaposes resources and a task listing, showing *who* is supposed to do *what*

Resource Gantt chart: A bar chart that shows how individual resources are allocated to tasks over time

Resource loading chart (histogram): A chart that shows the number of resources allocated to a project over time

Risk Management Tools

Risk assessment methodology: A three-step process that entails risk identification, risk impact analysis, and risk response planning

Scenario building: The analysis of possible project outcomes using a step-by-step approach that shows how one outcome might lead to another and how these outcomes might lead to others and so on

Monte Carlo simulation: A multi-iteration, statistical technique that estimates such things as budgets, task durations, and resource loadings

Basic statistical concepts: Procedures including mathematical expectation, expected monetary value, mean, mode, median, and standard deviation

Decision tree: A tree-shaped diagram in which each branch represents a possible course of action, with an associated probability of occurrence

Quality Management Tools

Standard quality control techniques: Methodologies including control charts and run charts

Pareto diagram: A chart that highlights the sources of problems leading to quality deficiencies

Contract Management Tools

There are no specific tools to master in this competency area. Project professionals should have a solid grasp of different contract modalities, however, including cost-plus-incentive-fee, cost-plus-award-fee, cost-plus-fixed-fee, firm-fixed-price, and time-and-materials approaches to contracting.

Communication Management Tools

There are no specific tools to master in this competency area. Project professionals, however, should understand the communication model that consists of sender, receiver, encoding, decoding, and feedback.

Project Management Certification

As mentioned earlier, in 1984 PMI developed a certification process to identify the degree to which project workers have mastered basic project management competencies. I directed PMI's certification effort from January 1990 until March 1996 and was privileged to witness its explosive growth during this period. In its first six years, from 1984 through 1989, the program certified an average of just under sixty people per year. Then, at the outset of 1990, AT&T began requiring its project managers to become certified Project Management Professionals (which is PMI's designation for individuals who have successfully passed its certification procedures). Other companies and government agencies quickly followed suit, including such prominent organizations as EDS, Citibank, Bell Atlantic, Asea Brown Boveri, IBM, Bell South, Bell Core, U.S. West, NCR, Lucent Technologies, Microsoft, Motorola, Hewlett-Packard, Allied Signal, GTE, the Defense Systems Management College, the federal courts, and the Department of Energy. Scores of smaller, vibrant companies also began requiring their employees to be certified. Certification efforts even migrated overseas, where prominent organizations in Australia, Singapore, France, the United Kingdom, Malaysia, Hong Kong, Russia, the Ukraine, Sweden, and Egypt encouraged their employees to go through the certification process.

I know from my own experience with the project management certification phenomenon that this growth was stimulated by three forces. First, once certification gained support from such organizations as AT&T, EDS, NCR, Asea Brown Boveri, and IBM, its rapid growth was ensured, because these organizations would be sending hundreds—in some cases, thousands—of their employees through the certification process. Second, PMI's local chapters recognized that if they promoted certification in their local regions, they had an appealing vehicle for attracting new membership. So they began advertising the virtues of certification to local companies and individuals and began offering certification preparation courses. Their strategies paid off, and project management certification boomed at the grassroots level. Third, individual men and women seized on certification as a way to increase their attractiveness to employers. Even when their organizations did not actively support project management certification, individuals pursued it on their own.

Achieving project management certification entails passing two reviews. One is a *qualification review*. Applicants are asked to provide detailed information about their educational and work backgrounds. To qualify to be certified, they must demonstrate that they have a basic level of educational and work experience. Details of the qualification requirement can be found on the PMI Web site at *www.pmi.org*. The second and better known review requires applicants to sit for a rigorous examination that assesses their mastery of project management competencies as outlined in *Guide to the PMBOK* (Duncan, 1996). The examination is structured in a multiple-choice format.

During my six years as director of certification, I was continually asked, Do you seriously believe that a multiple-choice examination can identify whether someone can function effectively as a project professional? My answer has been an unequivocal no! The theme of this book is that effective project management competencies are rooted in a variety of factors, a number of which simply cannot be identified by means of a multiple-choice exam. If that is the case, then what value does the certification exam have?

The exam does a good job of assessing the knowledge-based competencies of aspiring project professionals. Although a multiple-choice exam cannot assess whether the project professional's organization provides the needed support for project workers to operate effectively, and although it does not measure the political or empathetic skills of aspiring project professionals, it does assess whether they have the basic knowledge needed to do their jobs effectively. For example, individuals who purport to have the skills necessary to schedule projects properly should know how to calculate a critical path. In addition, they should certainly know the risk implications of carrying out a project with a cost-plus-fixed-fee contract, in contrast to executing a project operating under a firm-fixed-price contract. They should also have a thorough appreciation of the strengths and weaknesses of managing projects in a matrix environment, because the majority of projects entail use of borrowed resources—and so on. I believe that these knowledge-based competencies can be readily measured by means of a multiple-choice exam.

Readers of this book can develop some idea of whether they have the knowledge-based competencies to pass the PMI exam by taking the sample exam contained in Chapter Eight. The questions in the sample exam focus on the eight PMBOK areas covered on the full PMI exam. The sample exam has been designed to offer readers a sense of the real thing.

General Competencies

Guide to the PMBOK is specifically geared to identifying competencies that bear directly on project management. Mastery of *Guide to the PMBOK* competencies can serve project professionals well. Through such mastery they will grasp the tools, concepts, and vocabulary that are being employed in the project management community throughout the world.

Mastery of *Guide to the PMBOK* is not enough, however. There is also of course a range of knowledge-based skills beyond the competencies defined in *Guide to the PMBOK*. These skill requirements need to be developed in the context of an individual's work environment, but a number of general requirements can be postulated that apply to nearly all knowledge workers today. For example, when people undertake knowledge work, the assumption is that they are computer literate. This does not mean that they should be masters of the operating systems of mainframe computers. It does mean, however, that they should be adept at using word processors, have basic spreadsheet skills, be able to send and receive messages through e-mail, and be able to access the World Wide Web.

Another general knowledge-based capability that competent managers should possess is basic numeracy. Today's managers are surrounded by data. Many must deal with financial figures on a daily basis in order to compute costs, revenues, and profits. They may also be required to interpret financial data on net present value, internal rate of return, and payback period. Today's managers often must be capable of making personnel projections, which requires them to extrapolate future personnel requirements based on past labor usage. They need to know how to develop and interpret charts that present numerical data, and so on.

Certain litmus tests can be developed to identify whether managers have the basic mathematical knowledge to operate effectively in today's complex world. For example, managers who do not know the difference between a mean, a mode, and a median—and who see no value in learning about these statistical measures—may have a tough time understanding whether a statistical assessment they have just received is providing them with an accurate view of what is happening on a project.

Some key general competencies that are not project-specific are discussed in Chapters Six and Seven.

Conclusions

The competence of project professionals is reflected in a number of different dimensions. It is rooted in their grasp of the knowledge base, in their judgment, and in their ability to work with other people. This chapter has focused on knowledge-based competence.

Knowledge-based competence is associated with a clearly defined body of knowledge with which competent project professionals should be familiar. This core knowledge is captured in *Guide to the PMBOK*. A process exists to measure the extent to which individuals have mastered these PMBOK-related competencies: PMI's certification examination.

It is naive to think that mastery of a collection of techniques and concepts will guarantee effectiveness in project professionals. It does not take much imagination to picture a highly knowledgeable project worker failing on his projects because of poor social or business skills. Possession of a solid understanding of pertinent techniques and concepts is helpful, however, in providing individuals with the capabilities they need to solve problems. Given two equally capable people, the one who has mastered the core techniques and concepts will be able to operate more effectively on the job.

Chapter Five

Developing the Project Management Knowledge Base

On a number of occasions, when I have asked employees of project-focused organizations whether they know how to build spread-sheets, I have been answered in the following way: "No, I don't, because my company hasn't offered me any spreadsheet training." I find this answer to be enormously disheartening, because it suggests that the respondent believes that the only way to learn new methods is through formal training. *This simply is not true.* One trait of the most effective people in the work world is that they are constantly upgrading their education by whatever means are available. If they have an opportunity to learn by taking a course, so be it. If formal courses are not available, they teach themselves. They may go to a library or bookstore to acquire books that will provide them with the information they need. They may also try to identify people who possess the skills they seek and work with them to strengthen their capabilities.

This chapter examines various ways that people can build their knowledge-based competence, ranging from formal education and training to self-instruction to mentorship and on-the-job training. Before discussing the different avenues for gaining knowledge, however, I would like to explore a point that is obvious but often overlooked by people who aspire to strengthen their knowledge-based competence—that is, no amount of classroom education and book knowledge by itself is going to make individuals competent. Ultimately, the knowledge gained through study must be applied in practice if it is going to stick. Effective learning requires a commitment to achieving mastery through continual and often tedious practice.

The Need for Mastery

The dust jacket of Deepak Chopra's best-selling book *The Seven Spiritual Laws of Success* (1994) states, "Based on natural laws which govern all of creation, *this book shatters the myth that success is the result of hard work, exacting plans, or driving ambition*" (italics added). Of course this statement is nonsense. A review of the lives of successful people in all walks of life (including spiritual leaders) shows that one thing they have in common is that they work hard to achieve their success. What is frightening is that Chopra's book remained on the *New York Times* best-seller list for most of 1995 and 1996! Apparently a large number of people are willing to be deluded into believing that success can be achieved effortlessly.

Peter Senge's *Fifth Discipline* (1990) identifies *personal mastery* as one of the five key disciplines that people should seek. Although Senge is not precise in defining personal mastery, a key component is continual learning. People who achieve personal mastery have an insatiable appetite for knowledge and understanding. They never let up in their attempts to learn. The payoffs to such a duty to learning are substantial. According to Senge, "People with high levels of personal mastery are more committed. They take more initiative. They have a broader and deeper sense of responsibility in their work. They learn faster" (p. 143). These are people who add value to their organizations. The implications of Senge's observations are clear. First, organizations should seek to hire people with an innate propensity toward personal mastery. Second, they should strive to create working environments that nurture it.

In his study of what contributes to the effectiveness of people in the worlds of school and work, Daniel Goleman (1995) notes that mastery is a characteristic these people share. He also points out that the achievement of mastery entails a high degree of discipline and a long-term commitment to learning. Again, the payoffs are substantial. "What seems to set apart those at the very top of competitive pursuits from others of roughly equal ability is the degree to which, beginning early in life, they can pursue an arduous practice routine for years and years" (p. 81). In other words, if you want to be effective in your career, then you need to put your nose to the grindstone and commit yourself to learning over the long haul. Effective learning is a cumulative process, not one that is achieved in short bursts.

Both Senge's and Goleman's views were presaged in Thomas Edison's well-known statement that genius is 1 percent inspiration and 99 percent perspiration.

An operational consequence of mastery is that certain behavior becomes almost automatic. Through constant drilling, the people who have achieved mastery are able to make decisions on the basis of "instinct" rather than through ponderous analysis. This frees them to devote more time to dealing with exceptional problems. People who play the piano proficiently recognize this feature of mastery. Years of practice enable them to read music and play tunes without conscious effort. Similarly, coaches of sports teams recognize that the chief value of constant drills is to move the decisions made by their athletes from the realm of the conscious to the realm of the unconscious.

Effective learning requires people to take the knowledge they acquire in the classroom and through books and apply it in practice. If this knowledge is not practiced, it will quickly slip away. This reality is illustrated by an experience I recently had in which I came across a colleague who was swearing to herself while sitting at her computer. I asked her what the problem was. She answered, "Six months ago I took a one-day training course on using this word-processing software, but after the course I never worked with it. Now I'm trying to relearn my lessons and it's as if I never took the course at all."

The need to practice what is learned should be self-evident, but the enormous success of Chopra's book suggests that it is not.

Formal Education and Training

Through formal education and training, individuals acquire knowledge in a systematic fashion. The knowledge is conveyed by a person who is in some measure an authority on the subject matter being conveyed. Thus in university-level courses instructors are typically professors, the majority of whom possess doctoral degrees, indicating many years of study beyond the undergraduate degree. In an introductory C++ programming class the instructor presumably has extensive experience in programming in the C++ language and may have undergone substantial formal training in this area.

When we talk about education and training, we often highlight the difference between these two concepts. *Education* is generally seen to focus on acquiring knowledge in order to gain *understanding*. It places great stock in mastering theory. *Training*, in contrast, is seen to focus on acquiring knowledge to gain *skills*. It places great stock in mastering practice. We have all heard someone say, "You don't have to know the details of how an automobile works in order to drive a car." This statement is certainly correct. Through training (so-called driver's ed classes), individuals can learn how to operate automobiles without having the slightest idea of what goes on beneath a car's hood. If, however, one wants to design an automobile to function more effectively, then one certainly needs to be educated in a broad range of disciplines, including materials science, combustion engineering, principles of mechanical systems, and electronics.

Quite often the distinction between education and training is blurred. For example, it is common for universities today to offer academic courses designed to provide students with basic computer literacy skills. These courses are generally devoid of theoretical content. When they are offered as part of a college curriculum they are viewed as educational; when they are offered outside the university environment, however, they are labeled training courses.

Clearly, both education and training have important roles to play in developing knowledge-based competencies.

Acquiring Education

As stated, education is largely concerned with acquiring knowledge in order to gain an understanding of the hows and whys of life. Education is generally achieved through formal means—for example, by attending classes at an educational institution. With the advent of new teaching-delivery technology—such as CD-ROMs, video-based instruction, computer-assisted instruction, and Internet-based courseware—the traditional approach of having a lecturer stand before a classroom of eager students is likely to play a diminished role.

Formal education is typically associated with university-based instruction. The general perception is that a well-educated person is one who possesses a university degree of some sort. Not long ago an undergraduate university degree was viewed as a major achievement. Today increasing numbers of men and women pursue educational opportunities beyond the bachelor's degree, and master's degrees are now the sign of high educational achievement. The masochists among us can even go beyond the master's to obtain a doctorate.

In the project management arena, master's degrees specializing in project management have proliferated. I am often asked by men and women in the work world whether it makes sense for them to pursue a graduate degree in project management or some related discipline (such as contract management, systems engineering, or engineering management). Regrettably I do not have a standard answer to this question. My approach to answering it is to raise a number of my own questions. For example, I always ask, "Why do you feel it is necessary to obtain an advanced degree?" If the interlocutor answers, "To get a job promotion" or "To get an increase in salary," I find it difficult to encourage him or her to pursue a graduate degree on purely practical grounds. Tuition for courses is expensive. If the person is interested in accumulating wealth, he or she can take the money that would go to tuition and invest it in the stock of the next Microsoft Corporation. Furthermore, the burden of studying for courses will limit the time the person has to pursue other opportunities—both moneymaking and leisure-pursuing opportunities. All those evenings at the desk may in fact lead to alienation from the family.

Conversely, people who delight in gaining new insights and who want to pursue graduate education to strengthen their basic competencies—that is, people who aspire to Senge's and Goleman's concepts of mastery—can benefit enormously from graduate-level education. Not only will they broaden their knowledge base, but they will also learn how to raise the right questions to solve problems. A former doctoral student of mine who now runs multibillion-dollar aerospace projects recently told me that the chief value of his advanced educational study was that it taught him how to formulate problem statements so he can address complex problems in a relatively simple fashion. Interestingly, those who are educable and who learn their lessons well often gain substantial earthly rewards—money and recognition.

What kind of coursework should be pursued? Of course there is no simple answer to this question either. In selecting an educational program to follow, the future student should address a number of important questions:

- What educational shortcomings do I now have that can be strengthened?
- Is there a demand for people with the educational background I am striving to acquire? If so, will this demand exist ten years from now?
- How much money, time, and energy must I expend to achieve my educational goals? Could I dedicate these resources to other, more productive pursuits?
- Are my educational goals best achieved as a part-time student, or should I quit my job and enroll full-time?
- Does the educational institution in which I plan to enroll have any stature? If not, will its lack of stature diminish the value of my educational effort?
- Do I view the furtherance of my education as an exciting challenge that will help me grow as a person, or do I see it as a thankless chore?

By answering questions such as these, prospective students should be able to assess their degree of commitment to pursuing formal education. Without a high level of commitment, the educational experience will be expensive, unpleasant, and unproductive.

Acquiring Training

Training has become a popular and essential way for people to gain the skills they need in a fast-changing world. Certainly technological change requires that people continually be brought up to speed on the latest technical developments. Each time an organization changes its accounting systems, order-processing systems, or general management information systems; each time it acquires new equipment or software; each time it implements a new management initiative, such as Total Quality Management or just-in-time inventory control; and each time it hires new employees, a bevy of men and women must be trained. It is not uncommon for managers in high-performing organizations to undertake two or three weeks of training each year.

Training does not come cheaply. It often entails travel costs and living expenses in addition to tuition costs. Beyond this, the trainees are being paid salaries and fringe benefits even though they are away from their jobs—and of course their regular work must stop, or at least slow down, while they undergo training.

No one disputes the efficacy of training that focuses on clearly defined "technical" topics. For example, a company that produces new products would commit organizational suicide if it did not regularly train its sales staff on the latest features of its products. Similarly, it is inconceivable for an accounts receivable department to implement a new accounts receivable system without training staff on how to use the new system.

When training addresses broader issues—when it attempts to educate people on basic principles—its efficacy becomes more questionable. Consider, for example, training staff on the use of electronic spreadsheets. (My personal opinion is that spreadsheet software is the single most useful decision-support tool available to help project managers do their jobs.) I have witnessed a number of spreadsheet training classes. Typically they are composed of fifteen to twenty students working in a computer laboratory, with one student per computer workstation. Students usually range from secretaries to department heads. Generally the class focuses on learning rudimentary principles. For example, the first lesson may look at using spreadsheets to add numbers across columns. The second lesson may examine how to compute an average using the @AVG function, how to calculate a standard deviation using @STD, and how to compute internal rate of return using @IRR. Additional lessons may examine how spreadsheets can be employed to create databases, to generate impressive graphics, and to model financial processes. Regrettably, the examples employed in these classes are quite abstract and only marginally relevant to the students.

At the end of two days of instruction students are tested on their knowledge of spreadsheets by a quiz that asks them to compute an average, calculate a standard deviation, create a pie chart, and sort a list of telephone numbers. Both secretaries and department heads may score perfectly on their quizzes, but they may find it difficult to apply what they have learned in class to the circumstances they face on the job, so when they return home they may revert to business as usual.

Anyone who effectively uses spreadsheets recognizes that the real value of these tools lies in their ability to address business issues flexibly. People who are proficient in spreadsheet usage can see how a problem they encounter can be redefined in a context that lends itself to spreadsheet analysis. Unfortunately this kind of proficiency is not easily conveyed in spreadsheet usage courses.

A number of conditions must be met if training is to lead to desired results. First, the training material must be conveyed effectively. For example, notebooks, textbooks, and pertinent software must be understandable and palatable and must deal with relevant topics. The instructor must be a master of the subject and have good teaching skills. Second, students must be properly prepared to deal with the course material before the training begins. If the spreadsheet training course requires that students be familiar with the Microsoft Windows operating environment, then students who come to the course without the proper background may find themselves lost from the opening moments of class. Third, students must have a good aptitude (and attitude!) for learning. If they do not understand a point, they should feel free to ask questions. They should not be intimidated by the material. Good learners recognize that although some lessons come easily, others require substantial effort. If they are stuck on a particular point, they should not give up but should set aside time to study the point more carefully.

Finally, the best students are capable of extrapolating even the most mundane classroom exercises to real-world situations. In carrying out an exercise, for instance, to calculate the mean value of a column of numbers, Student A (who has problems using his imagination to think outside of his conceptual box) may react by saying, "What a waste of time! I don't plan to use spreadsheets to calculate averages." In contrast, Student B may see the true value of the exercise; by calculating the mean value of a column of numbers, he is learning how to perform operations on numbers in general and is now introduced to the use of spreadsheet-supplied functions that will prove useful in making financial, statistical, and mathematical computations.

The limitations of training should be clearly recognized. Even the best-conceived and best-implemented training program in the world will not produce miracles. Ultimately training should be viewed as an exercise in opening doors. Once the door is open, students can enter into a new room. What they do in the room—that is, whether they take advantage of its offerings or ignore them—is up to them. And even when students grasp their lessons well, they will not achieve true mastery of the material unless they apply the lessons over and over again in their work environment.

Self-Instruction

I was very fortunate in my first serious job. For seven years I worked in a research environment that put me in the midst of first-rate scientists—chiefly physicists and chemists. I am also fortunate to be the son and grandson of medical scientists. Regrettably, most people have little exposure to scientists in action. Their images of scientific pursuits are primarily derived from distorted portrayals created in Hollywood.

Competent project professionals can learn a great deal about effective problem solving if they understand how scientists go about their work. The reality of scientific research is that there are no template solutions to problems. No one provides scientists with answers to their questions on a silver platter. If you want an answer, you have to figure out how to find it. The spirit of scientific research is nicely captured in the Spanish word for research: *investigacion*. This word suggests that a scientist, like a detective, is involved in the process of discovery. The discoveries themselves are the consequences of probing and prodding. Scientists use whatever tools are available to them to carry out their investigations. If the proper tools do not exist, they may have to fabricate them. If they have deficiencies of knowledge, they remedy these deficiencies by self-study and by consulting knowledgeable people.

What I am suggesting here is that good scientists are enormously self-sufficient. After I joined a research organization filled with scientists, I learned this lesson in a dramatic way. I got the job because I had solid graduate-level education in multivariate statistics. My first assignment was to create a moderate-sized database that I would eventually analyze statistically. Because the research organization had a limited budget, I did not have access to the computing power of a mainframe computer (mainframe usage was an expensive proposition in the early 1970s). My boss told me that I should create the database using an on-line computer service—an affordable novelty at the time. He supplied me with a teletype terminal that used paper tape as the data storage medium. The problem I faced was that as a graduate student I had worked only with mainframe-based statistical packages and, first, I did not have a clue about how on-line remote-access computer systems worked, and second, I was not sure what was involved in database development.

When I expressed my concerns to my boss, who was trained as a nuclear chemist and had migrated into the computer science field, he responded, "No problem. Let's first get you up to speed on using the on-line system." He went to the blackboard he had in his office (all scientists had blackboards in their offices in the old days; today, they all have white boards) and roughly sketched out the architecture of the Honeywell computer system that served as the "engine" of our on-line service. Then he dialed up the computer, carried out a few simple operations, and concluded my "lesson." The tutorial had lasted about twenty minutes. "See, there's really nothing to it," he said with a smile.

"Now, about the database," he continued. "We're not looking for anything fancy. Just throw something together using FORTRAN IV."

When I told him that I had never programmed in FORTRAN, he responded. "Really? Let's take care of that." He rummaged through a pile of manuals on a nearby table, pulled one out, and handed it to me. It was an IBM technical manual describing the features of FORTRAN IV programming. "This manual should give you all the information you need. Any questions?"

I had plenty of questions, but concern about my job security dictated that I keep my mouth shut. Armed with my FORTRAN manual and a two-page brochure for accessing the Honeywell computer, I went off to my office to get "up to speed." Over the next three weeks I spent eighty hours per week educating myself to acquire the information I needed to do my job. Within a month I had created my first database.

The Key: Keep It Simple!

The ability to engage in effective self-instruction is a skill. As with any skill, there are both proper and improper ways to carry it out. As with any skill, it is learnable, and proficiency can be achieved through practice.

People who routinely educate themselves have learned that self-instruction requires them to keep the lessons as simple as possible. As a first shot in learning new material, they should find teaching sources that present the subject matter simply. In general, good, simple presentations are also relatively brief. The last thing the neophyte needs is study material that is lengthy, complex, and indigestible. It is easy to become frustrated by such material and to abandon the learning effort.

Students should test their mastery of concepts and tools by using simple examples. For instance, in practicing PERT chart development skills, why not create a scenario along the lines of "Scheduling the Smith Family's Picnic"? I have found that many students resist this approach because it does not accurately reflect the kinds of projects on which they work. It seems that they would rather test their PERT chart development skills on an example that requires them to schedule the construction of a nuclear power plant! My response to them is, "Start with scheduling a picnic. If you can't do that, then you don't have a chance in scheduling something more complex." Once students have mastered the basics through simple examples, they can then gradually turn their attention to more complex and realistic examples.

This is the approach that scientists take to solving problems. Einstein was well known for reducing complex problems to their simplest elements. His first step in understanding relativity occurred when, as a young man, he asked himself, "What would it be like to ride a beam of light?"

The ability of good scientists to keep things simple was illustrated dramatically by Noble Prize–winning physicist Richard Feynman during the hearings that investigated the Space Shuttle Challenger disaster. The immediate cause of the explosion of the Challenger was that the rubber O-ring on the external fuel tank had become brittle because the Challenger was launched in cold weather. At the hearings, a NASA official explained to the investigating panel that proper testing of the O-ring's sensitivity to cold temperatures was a complex undertaking. At this point Feynman took a segment of O-ring that was in front of him and dipped it into a glass of ice water. No words were necessary. The simplicity of his approach made the NASA position look foolish.

Traditional Resources: Books and Articles

There is an abundance of resources that men and women can employ to help them in their quest to learn through self-instruction.

General management works. The primary traditional sources of information have been books and journal articles. Consequently, a good first step in teaching oneself new skills would be to visit the local library and bookstore. If the goal of self-instruction is to develop stronger knowledge-based project management competencies, a good starting point would be to read works dealing with general management topics. In my view, almost anything written by Peter Drucker is worthwhile. My personal favorite is *The Effective Executive* (1967). It is attractive because it is short, it captures the essence of Drucker's overall philosophy, it offers practical advice, and it is inspiring.

The self-instructed student should also lay hands on a work that describes today's key management concerns. There are many such books from which to choose. My personal favorites are Charles Handy's *The Age of Unreason* (1989) and *The Age of Paradox* (1994). Like Drucker, Handy has a knack for focusing on the real issues of concern for today's managers, and his books are highly readable.

Project management war stories. A rich source of insights into the realities of project management is books that offer "war stories" on projects that have been carried out. Many such books exist, describing everything from building bridges to designing computers to creating complex weapons systems. These books are the self-instructed student's equivalent of Harvard Business School's famous case studies. By reading them, students can experience projects vicariously. They can witness project disasters without having their teeth kicked out. Similarly, they can feel the excitement of success when a project is brought in on time, within budget, and according to specifications.

For students desiring specific recommendations of good experience-focused books, I suggest the following works:

• Frederick P. Brooks Jr., *The Mythical Man-Month* (1975). As noted earlier, Brooks was the project manager for the development of the operating system of IBM's 360 computer. He is regarded as one of the most effective project managers around. This book, based on his experiences at IBM, provides guidance from an articulate and experienced professional on how to carry out projects effectively.

• Ben R. Rich and Leo Janos, *Skunk Works* (1994). This work was written by the former director of Lockheed's Skunk Works, an organization that undertook some of the most sophisticated high-technology aerospace projects ever pursued. The book highlights the efforts of the Skunk Works' founder, Kelly Johnson, certainly one of the most capable project managers in history.

• Patrick Tyler, *Running Critical* (1986). This book describes the ugly interactions between the Navy, Hyman Rickover, and General Dynamics' Electric Boat division in the production of Los Angeles Class submarines. Ultimately, politics and illegal activities contributed to some of the largest cost overruns ever encountered in defense contracts.

• Tracy Kidder, *The Soul of a New Machine* (1981) and *House* (1985). Kidder is a Pulitzer Prize–winning journalist who in these two books takes an anthropological approach to describing project activity. In *The Soul of a New Machine* he describes the heroic effort of young engineers to build a high-performing minicomputer under trying conditions. In *House* he describes the building of a house from beginning to end. In both works, Kidder provides excellent insights into the role of people in projects.

Project management texts. Project management texts serve two functions for individuals attempting to strengthen their knowledge-based competencies. First, they can provide readers with step-by-step instructions to learn project management skills. To serve this function effectively, the texts should be readable and clear. Many texts fail this test. They are overly long and complex and present project management as if it were an advanced engineering discipline—which it is not. Second, they can be reference works, such as an encyclopedia, that provide project professionals with detailed information on technical topics such as alternative scheduling algorithms and project selection techniques. Students may find it difficult to locate a single project management text that satisfies both of these functions. In such a case, it behooves them to get their hands on two or more texts.

A word of warning on choosing a project management text: before purchasing one, review it to make sure that its contents reflect today's project realities. As I discuss in detail in *The New Project Management* (1994), today's realities include such phenomena as downsizing, outsourcing, flattened organizations, empowerment, and customer focus. Managing projects today is clearly about *business management*. Too many works, however, view project management from the perspectives of the 1950s and 1960s and see it fundamentally as a technical process in which the project team's job is simply to implement solutions provided to it. The old-fashioned character of some texts is even reflected in the treatment of project management tools. Quite a few texts still teach project management using arrow diagram network charts (the dominant approach from the 1950s through the 1970s), yet practically none of today's scheduling software supports this approach, employing instead the precedence diagram method of scheduling.

Traditional Self-Instruction Using New Technology

Given recent technological advances, students are not restricted to gaining information through the print media. Increasingly they can carry out traditional studies using such technologies as CD-ROMs, videocassettes, audiocassettes, and Internet-based instruction. Although the technology is new, the basic learning process is quite traditional. Students read text (CD-ROMs, the Internet), listen to guidance (audiocassettes), and view demonstrations (videocassettes, CD-ROMs, the Internet) in a fashion that parallels the traditional approaches of reading books and sitting in classrooms. The availability of study material provided through today's technology is increasing explosively.

Self-Instruction Using Computerized Software Tools

Aficionados of self-education who are also computer literate have discovered that applications software is a great instructor, enabling students to engage in *active learning* experiences. The traditional self-instruction techniques just described entail passive learning. By using applications software (such as spreadsheets, project-scheduling software, Monte Carlo simulators), students can roll up their sleeves and get their hands dirty as they teach themselves all manner of management and analytical techniques, such as capital budgeting, PERT/CPM network construction, and benefit-cost analysis.

There are two reasons applications software is an attractive teaching tool. First, software vendors assume that their audience's knowledge of the topic is limited, so they supply relatively friendly introductions to the topic in user manuals and also provide step-by-step tutorials. In addition, third-party vendors often produce how-to manuals (sold in bookstores and computer stores) that offer detailed guidance on how to employ the most popular brands of software. These manuals are in effect textbooks.

This point can be shown by means of some illustrations:

• Myra wants to teach herself basic capital budgeting techniques. She will use Super Spreadsheet (a fictitious product) as her instructor. Super Spreadsheet contains financial functions that enable analysts to compute present value and internal rate of return. The Super Spreadsheet manual contains a brief description of what these techniques do and also shows how to carry out a net-present-value and internal-rate-of-return analysis on the spreadsheet. In addition, Myra buys a manual prepared by a third-party publisher on how to use Super Spreadsheet; it offers a detailed treatment of Super Spreadsheet's power in conducting financial analyses.

• Myron wants to teach himself basic project management scheduling, budgeting, and resource allocation techniques. He purchases Super Scheduler (a fictitious product) as his instructor. The user manual comes with a fifty-page overview of project management principles. A third-party vendor has published a how-to-use-Super-Scheduler manual that Myron finds very helpful.

• Marsha has been assigned to work with a risk management team in her organization and is expected to have a working knowledge of Monte Carlo simulation. She obtains a copy of Super Risk software (a fictitious product) from the risk management group. During a weekend, she goes through the Monte Carlo simulation tutorial. By Monday morning she has a basic grasp of Monte Carlo simulation principles and is able to apply this knowledge to risk assessments of project cost estimates.

A second attractive feature of applications software as a teaching tool is that it offers students hands-on learning experience. Traditional classroom and book-based instruction usually entail passive learning. Students absorb information by listening and reading, but do not put their knowledge to much practice (aside from some fairly superficial homework assignments). In contrast, mastering the use of a software package involves active learning, which in turn stimulates stronger student involvement in the learning process. As a consequence, the lessons tend to stick.

Apprenticeship

An age-old approach to learning skills is through apprenticeship. In Europe, virtually all craft skills in medieval times were developed by apprenticing sycophants to a master. The master would play a mentoring role and the student would learn by doing.

This is still a good way to gain skills, though it is not necessary to enter into a formal apprenticeship arrangement. When students recognize that they need to develop new skills, they should approach someone who already possesses knowledge of the skills and ask for some guidance from them. This need not require a major commitment of time on the part of the selected mentor. Often the educational experience may simply entail the mentor's stepping through a process briefly and explaining it to the student. The student can learn by observing the walk-through and questioning the mentor. As the student goes through the steps of the process, the mentor can critique the student's performance and offer pointers. For this approach to work, it is important that the mentor be available for feedback when the student first attempts to apply the newly gained knowledge.

A particularly attractive feature of this approach is that it is flexible and enables people to pick up skills as they need them. If we want to give a modern name to this old idea, we can call it just-in-time training.

Conclusions

Modern management theory and practice correctly recognize the significance of learning and mastery for the effective functioning of people and organizations. Knowledge is growing at an exponential rate. As some old wise person once put it, the only constant is change. Individuals and organizations that do not continually upgrade their knowledge-based skills will quickly grow obsolete.

As with other professions, project management practice is based on a core body of knowledge that is changing day by day. Project professionals who desire to be effective and to receive high rewards for their efforts need to take steps to keep up with the latest insights and tools. Although some of this knowledge can be gained through formal means (such as in the classroom), project professionals are increasingly expected to maintain their skills and insights through self-study.

Chapter Six

Developing People Management Skills
The Soft Side of Project Management

In the mid-1970s I had the dubious distinction of being screamed at by an internationally renowned physicist. My company was in the last stages of negotiating a sole-source contract with the Defense Department when we received notice that the division we were dealing with had just acquired a new director—the highly accomplished physicist. A colleague and I were asked to provide a briefing on our proposed project to the new director. This was no inconvenience to us because we routinely conducted such briefings.

When we arrived, the new director was sitting at the head of a table. He had a terrible scowl on his face. We were introduced to him, after which my colleague launched the briefing by describing the problem we were addressing. Then he stated that we would be using an eigenvalue formulation to solve the problem.

At this point—perhaps two minutes into the briefing—the new director slammed his hand against the table. "I know what an eigenvalue formulation is!" he screamed. "Do you think I don't know what an eigenvalue formulation is? I understand you contractors! You're just trying to do a snow job on us. You're trying to impress us with fancy talk."

With that he ended the meeting. He knew nothing about us or our capabilities. His attitude was governed solely by a stereotypical image of how government contractors operate. Our proposed project was killed on the spot. About ten months of preparatory work went down the drain.

Years later I met some people who had been working in the division when the new director arrived. I asked how things went with him as the head person. They responded that it was hell. The director specialized in public humiliations. No one dared stand up to him. The managers in the division quickly learned that in order to survive they had to tell him stories he liked to hear—which just goes to show that even technically accomplished prodigies can have deplorable human relations skills.

All of us have experienced situations in which we have encountered people with "book smarts" who lack common sense and what is commonly called "people skills." For example, many of us have worked with the technical genius we hide from customers because he invariably insults them, or the generally capable project manager who kills her project when she makes a long-winded, rambling presentation to senior management on the project's future prospects, or the office director with a twenty-year track record of excellent performance who destroys his career by making a single off-color joke as a keynote speaker at a minor conference.

Clearly, if we are concerned with assessing the competence of individuals to perform their jobs effectively, we must take into account more than their knowledge-based competence. We must assess their social competence as well. Yet even this is not enough. When examining the competence of project professionals, we must recognize that they operate in an environment in which they must continually make decisions that make good business sense. For example, effective project professionals make decisions that consistently reflect a weighing of costs against benefits. They recognize that in general they should avoid decisions that create costs that are greater than the benefits they generate. Unfortunately there are plenty of project workers who have mastered the art of scheduling tasks and who have good social skills yet who still make terrible business decisions. Such people lack a measure of business competence to carry out projects effectively.

This and the next chapter examine two areas of competence that lie outside the traditional realm of knowledge-based competence. This chapter reviews social competence and focuses on identifying the kinds of social skills that are needed to carry out projects effectively. The next chapter examines business competence, highlighting the basic business insights that effective project professionals should possess.

The Need for Social Skills

In the past twenty-five years I have met thousands of people employed in hundreds of organizations. I have worked either directly or indirectly on hundreds of projects. During this time *I have never encountered a project that failed because a PERT/CPM scheduling system crashed!* However, I have encountered countless failures rooted in people problems.

Competent project professionals must be able to balance "hard" and "soft" skills. The hard skills are much easier to deal with than the soft ones. It is a relatively simple matter to teach people how to calculate the critical path on a PERT chart. It is also easy to test them to see whether they have learned their lessons. It is much more difficult to teach people how to mediate conflicts on a project team or to motivate borrowed human resources to work sixty-hour weeks. Furthermore, it is difficult to assess whether they can actually apply their lessons in practice.

In view of the large number of project disasters that have been rooted in people problems, it is important to identify whether prospective project professionals possess the social competencies needed to perform their work effectively. Unfortunately, no clear-cut way to measure such competencies has been discovered. Instructors can always devise paper-and-pencil examinations to see whether students have learned their behavioral theory well. They can even base these exams on case studies in order to simulate real-world situations that project professionals may encounter. Even so, the results of such tests are a bit suspicious because a paper-based case study cannot simulate the actual pressures that decision makers face on the job. The best case studies are pale shadows of the real world.

If you are wary of paper-based examinations, you can attempt to assay the social competence of prospective project professionals through a rigorous interview process. The attraction of face-to-face interviews is that the interviewers have a firsthand opportunity to observe the interviewees' social skills. But those of us who have gone through such processes recognize that the impressions we develop of the interviewed candidates reflect the candidates' interviewing skills as much as their capability to handle real-world people problems on the job. We all know stories in which the prospective CEO of a company is given a job offer after going through extensive interviews with employees, members of management, human resource consultants, and members of the board of directors, only to fail miserably on the job.

This chapter examines the social competence that project managers and workers need if they hope to function effectively in their jobs. It sees social competence as closely tied to the development of good interpersonal and intrapersonal skills. In staffing key management positions on projects, senior managers should recognize that it is as important for prospective staff to possess solid interpersonal and intrapersonal skills as it is for them to have good knowledge-based competencies.

Gardner's Multiple Intelligences

In 1983, Howard Gardner published a book, *Frames of Mind,* that has had a major impact on how we view intelligence. As noted in Chapter Two, Gardner poses the view that human intelligence in fact consists of seven intelligences: musical, bodily-kinesthetic, spatial, logical-mathematical, linguistic, interpersonal, and intrapersonal. This diversity explains why people who are geniuses in the realm of music might be average in logical reasoning, or why people who are mathematically brilliant may have trouble finding their car in the parking lot of a supermarket.

Only two of these intelligences are measured by standard intelligence tests (IQ tests): logical-mathematical intelligence and linguistic intelligence. Research shows that IQ scores predict, in a rough sense, only the academic performance of individuals. They are not strongly correlated with career performance. This suggests that hiring a worker with a high IQ or good school grades offers no assurance that he or she will perform effectively on the job.

In the mid-1990s, Gardner's theory reached a broad audience through the publication of Daniel Goleman's best-seller *Emotional Intelligence* (1995). Building on Gardner's work, Goleman believes that the key intelligences that predict effective functioning in the workplace are interpersonal intelligence and intrapersonal intelligence. Interpersonal intelligence is concerned with the skills necessary to deal with other people. A fact of organizational life is that if one wants to achieve one's goals, one must obtain the cooperation of other people. This requires some measure of people skills.

The idea that interpersonal intelligence is important for management is not new. In 1962, Chris Argyris dedicated a whole book, *Interpersonal Competence and Organizational Effectiveness,* to the proposition that interpersonal competence is a key factor leading to managerial effectiveness.

Intrapersonal intelligence is the ability of individuals to understand themselves. Only by doing so can they begin to deal with their emotions and motivate themselves to achieve their goals.

The Importance of Interpersonal Intelligence in Project Management

A distinguishing characteristic of humans is that we are social animals. The success of the species is largely tied to this fact. Humans advance by cooperating with one another. Collectively we can achieve things that no one individual can accomplish alone. Given the social nature of humankind, it is obvious that possessing interpersonal skills is important if one wants to operate effectively in society.

One of the key traits of people with good interpersonal skills is their ability to empathize with others. Empathy is the capacity to put oneself into someone else's shoes. It underlies the Golden Rule: do unto others as you would have them do unto you. By being able to put oneself into other people's shoes, the individual is able to develop an understanding of the impact of his or her actions on others. For example, Martha meets George in the hallway and is astonished by his haggard appearance. She blurts out, "Lord, you look terrible, George." Such a comment suggests a momentary lack of empathy skills. No one likes to be told they look terrible. Conceivably George could take this comment in a lighthearted fashion and respond, "I not only look terrible, but I feel terrible as well. I was up all night working on the Whambangatron project." But if George is sensitive to Martha's comment, he might mutter to himself, "After putting in an all-nighter on the Whambangatron project, the last thing I need is to be insulted by a colleague."

People who are devoid of empathy skills are in some sense social misfits. A key trait of psychotics, for example, is their inability to visualize the effects of their actions on their victims. The psychotic who physically tortures a victim is unable to feel the victim's pain. More familiar in the office setting are people suffering from dyssemia, a condition, noted in Chapter Three, in which individuals are unable to read verbal and nonverbal cues directed at them by their colleagues. The man who continues to relate off-color jokes even while his audience responds with an embarrassed silence suffers from dyssemia. Strong empathy skills are a valuable asset for project professionals working in today's people-focused world. In particular, project professionals must be sensitive to the perspectives of their customers, their fellow project team members, and their management.

The Need for Empathy in Dealing with Customers

If a project team desires to produce a deliverable that leads to customer delight, then team members must be sensitive to the concerns and wants of their customers. Without empathy skills, they may find themselves in an us-versus-them situation. Without empathy skills, project teams simply cannot discern what it takes to satisfy customers. Consider the following two situations that commonly occur on projects and that require strong empathy skills on the part of project team members.

Every time customers review progress on the project, they request additions to the deliverable, thereby expanding the scope of the effort. This is a common experience on projects and goes by the name *learning effect.* As customers see what is being produced and achieve a better understanding of its capabilities, they develop new ideas of what the deliverable should look like and what it should do. Without empathy skills, we may react to customers' continual requests for change with a sense of frustration and ask, Why can't they make up their minds?

Empathetic project professionals recognize that the learning effect is natural and inevitable. Because of their empathy skills, they realize that when customers initially approve project requirements, they do not really know what they will be getting because their perception of the deliverable is rather abstract at this point. As the project proceeds, however, and the deliverable becomes more concrete, customers have a better understanding of what they will be getting and now have a solid basis for requesting adjustments. Recognizing the source of customers' apparent indecision, project professionals with good empathy skills can reduce their feelings of frustration about indecisive customers and prepare themselves to deal with change requests effectively.

Although customers hold us to tight deadlines, they often contribute to project delays by being slow in reviewing material submitted to them by the project team and slow in providing approvals to the team to move ahead with its work. This is a frequent occurrence on projects and causes project team members to feel that their customers have a double standard: they expect the team to maintain a schedule, but they feel no compunction to meet their own schedule obligations. A superficial reading of this phenomenon may lead team members to believe that their customers are disorganized procrastinators. The empathetic project professional, however, recognizes that the delayed turnaround of approvals may reflect political struggles in the customer organization. This occurs, for example, if the customer organization has several contending camps that do not have a harmonious view of what the project is supposed to accomplish. Delays can occur as the project sponsors in the customer organization work with their colleagues to get their support to move ahead with project activities.

The Need for Empathy in Dealing with Project Team Members

The effective management of a project team requires that project managers possess highly developed social skills. Teams are composed of people who each possess unique insights, aspirations, skills, and attitudes. A prime challenge of managing a team is to get the team members to play down their differences so they can work together harmoniously. If project managers lack empathy skills, they will not be able to understand the concerns of the team members, so they will not be able to address them.

The fact that most projects are carried out by using borrowed resources (matrix management) creates special problems for project managers. Consider the following list of problems associated with matrix management:

- The team members are typically assigned to the project—seldom do they volunteer to join it.

- While team members work on a project, their performance appraisals are usually made by their functional managers, who cannot directly monitor their project-related activities.
- During the course of a project, team members may have concurrent work assignments on other projects.
- While the team members are away on project assignments, they may lose opportunities for professional advancement back in their functional departments.
- Every time team members join a new team, they must spend a substantial amount of effort getting up to speed on what is transpiring on the project; they are seldom able to hit the ground running.

Project managers who are insensitive to the matrix-related conditions facing their team members may develop hostile feelings toward them. They may be angered by the fact that team members do not give 100 percent of their effort to the project—which is difficult for individuals who are assigned to multiple projects. They may be disgusted with the fact that new team members consume the project manager's time trying to identify what the team members' responsibilities are. (A common project manager complaint is, "These people are supposed to be experts; why don't they know what it takes to do their jobs?") They may be irritated by the team members' continual anxiety about life back in their functional departments. These feelings and this lack of empathy will contribute to project managers' inability to forge a sense of strong team spirit.

The Need for Empathy in Dealing with Management

Project professionals with empathy skills recognize the challenges that managers above them in the organization continually encounter. They know that their managers likely feel overwhelmed by the demands of the job. They understand that a substantial portion of the project professional's job is to make the manager's job easier.

Empathetic project professionals have a relatively easy time gaining support from their management. Because they recognize the constraints under which their managers operate, they do not make outrageous requests for resources. In making their requests, they carefully prepare solid arguments that address the key concerns of their managers. For example, if management is concerned with reducing costs, project professionals emphasize the cost-saving nature of their proposed solutions. If management is chiefly concerned with increasing profitability, project professionals show how their solutions generate profit.

Project professionals who lack empathy skills often add to their managers' burdens. They bring problems to management, not solutions. In making reports, they may provide more data than necessary—an act, incidentally, that contributes to micromanagement, because managers often manage their workers at whatever level of detail the workers supply them with information. Because non-empathetic project professionals are insensitive to the concerns of management, they may engender feelings of hostility among powerful people and find that they do not receive the upper-level support they need to do their jobs properly.

The Importance of Intrapersonal Intelligence in Project Management

Intrapersonal intelligence is associated with the old admonition, Know thyself! Walters and Gardner (1986, pp. 172–173) define it as "the access to one's own feeling life, one's range of emotions, the capacity to effect discrimination among these emotions, and eventually to label them and to draw upon them as a means of understanding and guiding one's own behavior."

Goleman (1995) sees intrapersonal intelligence leading to self-control and self-motivation, key psychological factors that bring success in the work world. He states, "Emotional self-control—delaying gratification and stifling impulsiveness—underlies accomplishment of every sort" (p. 43). He believes that impulsiveness is a curse that holds people back in their careers. "There is perhaps no psychological skill more fundamental than resisting impulse" (p. 81).

Empirical evidence backs up this perspective. A study carried out at Stanford University suggests that kids who demonstrate impulsive behavior as preschoolers grow up to be people who are not very effective socially. In contrast, those who resist their impulses as kids tend to operate more effectively as adults (Shoda, Mischel, and Peake, 1990).

There are at least two key consequences of intrapersonal intelligence. One is that it is necessary to have a measure of intrapersonal intelligence if one is to develop the all-important empathy skills discussed earlier. The other key consequence is that by possessing solid intrapersonal skills one is able to assess one's strengths and weaknesses and to use this knowledge to function more effectively in the social world.

Developing Intrapersonal Skills and Empathy

As discussed earlier, one of the most significant social skills that project professionals can possess is the capacity for empathy. Empathy skills allow them to feel what the people they deal with feel, enabling them to respond appropriately to meeting the needs and wants of their customers, team members, and managers.

A little reflection shows that empathy cannot be developed without self-knowledge. Empathetic individuals are able to put themselves into the shoes of other people. This entails a process of *visualizing* what others are going through and putting this information into a personal context. People with strong intrapersonal skills continually ask themselves, "How would *I* feel about these circumstances? How would *I* react to this situation?" People with weak intrapersonal skills are unable to define the personal context and consequently will lack strong interpersonal skills.

Understanding One's Strengths and Weaknesses

Project management is obsessed with achieving results. Project staff are under strong pressure to show themselves to be "can do" individuals. When a high-level manager says to an individual, "You can do that ten-month task in six months, can't you?" the individual may feel compelled to answer, "Sure, I can!" Yet if it truly is a ten-month task, or if the individual simply lacks the ability to carry out a superhuman effort, failure is built into the undertaking.

People with strong levels of intrapersonal intelligence know what their strengths and limitations are. Given this knowledge, they will be reluctant to commit themselves to solutions that lead to failure. Conversely, by knowing their strengths they may be able to push the organization to stretch itself and produce goods and services that lie outside its historical realm of operation.

The key point here is that a good understanding of one's strengths and weaknesses allows one to develop a realistic sense of what one is capable of achieving. People with solid intrapersonal insights are unlikely to establish unrealistic expectations among their customers, team members, and management.

Specific Project Management Social Competencies

A number of specific social competencies are sought in project professionals. These competencies are reflected in important social skills that effective project professionals should possess, including teamwork skills, political skills, diversity skills, communication skills, and listening skills.

Teamwork Skills

The concept of teamwork is one of today's hottest management buttons. An enormous literature has arisen on teamwork, focusing on its importance and proferring guidance on how to achieve it. The attention that teamwork is receiving is a consequence of the dramatic changes in the last few years in how organizations carry out their business. The forces that have led to such phenomena as downsizing, outsourcing, flattening, and empowerment have also compelled organizations to recognize that the old top-down hierarchical command-and-control systems no longer work. Teamwork is now seen as an effective way to offer viable solutions to problems in a complex world. Although the discussion of teamwork offered in this chapter is brief, team competency is discussed in detail in Chapters Nine and Ten.

Teamwork competency boils down to a simple proposition: *knowing how to work with others.* The ability to work with others is not always easy to achieve in Western culture, where the value of the individual is emphasized and teamwork is easily dismissed as an exercise in "groupthink." For individuals to be competent in the area of teamwork, they must believe in the following proposition: *Teams enable us to do things we simply cannot accomplish by working alone.*

A number of traits characterize people who have good teamwork skills:

- They have the capacity to pull back at the right time; although they may argue their positions strongly, when it becomes obvious that the team's emerging consensus rejects their position, they bow to the will of the team.

- They have the capacity to contribute actively to proposed solutions; effective team members are not excessively shy wallflowers who observe others debate the important issues from a safe vantage point and contribute nothing to the discussion.
- If they have assumed a leadership role on the team,

  - They are good at motivating borrowed resources, over whom they have little control.
  - They possess good facilitation skills that enable them to draw out the best insights of the team members.
  - They possess good conflict resolution skills that enable them to deal effectively with the different viewpoints held by their team members.

- They are comfortable dealing with diverse perspectives; they recognize that each team member has his or her unique view on how the world works and on how problems should be resolved, and they see this diversity in outlook as a strength rather than as a hassle.

Political Skills

As Robert Block points out in *The Politics of Projects* (1984), politics is the art of influence. It is not the art of sleaze and corruption. (As an old Washington hand who has lived in the District of Columbia for thirty years, I jokingly tell my students that sleaze and corruption are the *rewards* of political action, not the principal mechanism.) Project workers who eschew politics because they see it as an inherently dirty activity will have problems achieving their goals.

As has been noted, most projects are carried out in a matrixed structure, which means that project managers are working with borrowed resources. Because they are borrowed, project managers have little or no direct control over them. So how do project managers make their will prevail? By *influencing* borrowed team members, not by *commanding* them.

Effective project professionals know how to influence people—their team members, their customers, and their management.

They recognize that politics is not an inherently dirty enterprise but rather an inevitable feature of operating in organizations with limited resources.

Diversity Skills

Two of the greatest intellectual products of the nineteenth century were Charles Darwin's *On the Origin of Species by Means of Natural Selection* ([1859] 1979) and *The Descent of Man, and Selection in Relation to Sex* ([1871] 1989). These books were a paean to diversity. Darwin pointed out that evolution is a process whereby contending forces arising in an environment of diversity engage in a process of "natural selection" in which those best suited to a given environment survive and those not suited perish. Evolution, then, is largely a process of adjusting to changing environments, and the mechanism that makes this possible is diversity.

In the United States the word *diversity* has become a code word for the policy of affirmative action. Affirmative action programs thrived in the 1970s and 1980s and were designed to rectify some of the historical inequities caused by racial and sexual discrimination. In affirmative action programs, special preferences were given to hiring people from groups that had been discriminated against over the years.

In the late 1980s and early 1990s, many U.S. companies and government agencies implemented so-called diversity programs whose chief objective was to increase the representation of racial minorities and women in the work force. This effort has led to some confusion over the longstanding meaning of the term *diversity*. I recently found myself in a situation in which I had spent several minutes lecturing a class on the importance of diversity in generating stronger solutions to problems when one of my students said, "Let me see if I understand your point here. You're saying that it's important to hire minorities on projects, right?"

Although I support the hiring of minorities in organizations, *this is not what I had been saying.* My point is quite simple. We know that biological diversity enables species to strengthen themselves. If in a species there are some members who possess the ability to resist a particular disease, they will survive a debilitating epidemic and will ensure that future generations of the species can survive a particular threat. If the species lacks such disease-resistant members (that is, lacks diversity in this respect), it will perish.

Similarly, cross-functional teams in organizations reflect diversity in the organization's outlook. If a project team is composed of representatives from the marketing, information technology, operations, finance, and research and development departments, the solutions it generates are likely to be more robust than solutions generated by a team comprising only marketing people. To the extent that organizations can capitalize on their diversity to create cross-functional solutions to problems, they will grow stronger.

It is important for project professionals to possess the ability to understand, nurture, and employ diverse perspectives on their project efforts. This is not always easy to do, because to a certain extent we all wear blinders that restrict our outlooks. These blinders often come in the form of stereotypes. For example, a technically focused project manager who views salespeople as superficial money-grubbers may fail to recognize that the organization's sales staff has insights that can lead to improvements in the technical design of a product.

Communication Skills

The importance of communication skills in carrying out project work cannot be overemphasized. Consider the central role of effective communication in the following areas:

- Articulating needs and requirements
- Establishing realistic expectations—of customers, team members, and management
- Providing status updates of project progress
- Requesting resources
- Writing documents—memos, proposals, progress reports, technical reports

We all recognize that the best idea in the world has little value unless it is communicated properly. We also recognize that *the facts do not speak for themselves,* despite the age-old admonition to the contrary. Clearly communication skills are needed if important points are to be conveyed to an audience.

It is certainly helpful for project professionals to be good at communicating their points both orally and in writing. The requirement to express themselves orally is constant. In a typical day they convey instructions to team members, make management briefings, and update clients on project progress. If their instructions are unclear, team members may misunderstand them and do the wrong work. If their management briefings are long-winded and off the point (a common experience), they will not gain the management support they need. If they gloss over problems in their discussions with clients, they may be setting false expectations that may come back to haunt them later on.

The possession of good writing skills is equally important. Project professionals should be good wordsmiths and should also possess good editorial skills in order to discern whether the work being produced by the team is well written. Written documents are an outward and visible reflection of views and capabilities. They can be seen as a window into people's minds. A poorly written document—one that is not properly researched, is logically inconsistent, and contains rambling sentences, bad spelling, and poor punctuation—mirrors sloppy thinking. Readers of the document will rightly question the capabilities of the people who produced it.

In project management, an especially important communication skill is the capacity to deliver good briefings. Briefings are an important communication vehicle that keeps management informed of project progress. Higher-level managers are generally overwhelmed with data, so when they receive information in a palatable format, they take note of this fact. Briefings that are well received by higher levels of management lead to stronger degrees of support for the project. Poorly delivered briefings have the opposite effect: they diminish management support and may doom the project to failure.

Project professionals delivering an important briefing should recognize that the image they project is as important as the content of the briefing. By saying this I am not encouraging project professionals to behave superficially. What I am saying is that the image that managers take away from the briefing will be more enduring than recognition that throughput increased by 17.8 percent.

In a time when competence really counts, the most effective images conveyed are those that show the project team to be capable. A concise, to-the-point briefing that focuses on the real issues demonstrates to management that this team knows what it is doing. When during the briefing the presenter is queried by management, he or she should be able to answer questions confidently and show a mastery of the material.

It seems that everyone acknowledges the importance of good written and oral communication skills for the effective management of projects. The good news is that it is reasonably easy to test individuals to see whether they possess these skills. For example, prospective project managers might be asked to present a five-minute briefing on the value of Gantt charts as scheduling tools. In making this presentation, do they identify the key issues? How readily do they stick to the point? Do they have an engaging delivery that keeps the audience's attention? Do they have their facts straight?

Similar tests can be created to assess basic writing capabilities. For example, a prospective project manager might be asked to write a one- or two-page analysis of a short case study (this is an assignment that my MBA students are routinely given). Questions that should be addressed include, Is the analysis well developed? Do ideas flow together logically? Has the writer identified the key issues? Is the argument convincing? Is the piece grammatically correct?

The bad news is that despite recognizing the importance of effective communication skills, few organizations I have worked with give them the same weight as, say, the ability of a project professional to create a PERT chart. To me this is the height of folly. For every hour that project professionals spend working on PERT charts, they likely spend scores of hours communicating with their managers, their customers, and their team members.

Listening Skills

Effective communication is a two-way street. For people to communicate points meaningfully, they must be receptive to inputs and feedback from the world around them. Specifically, they must possess good listening skills.

Recently a distraught student rushed into my office like a whirlwind. She looked panic-stricken, as if she were being chased by demons. She related to me how worried she was about writing a paper for me that was due the following week. The more she worked on the paper, the less she knew what she should be doing.

As a university professor, I had run into this situation before. I had experienced it myself as an undergraduate student. However, the assignment I had given was not particularly challenging. The key to addressing it was to identify a handful of core issues. I decided to help this student by telling her what the core issues were. It would then be her job to take these insights and develop them into a cogent paper.

Providing guidance to this student turned out to be very difficult because *she completely lacked the capacity to listen.* Each time I tried to make a point, she would interrupt me. During a ten-minute "discussion" I don't think she allowed me to complete one sentence. I even tried to communicate with her using mental telepathy, directing mental messages to her, such as, "Listen to me, for heaven's sake, because I am giving you the answer to the assignment!" But these signals were rebuffed. In the end I gave up. Life will treat this student roughly. No doubt she will attribute her failures to the hostile actions of a tough world, but the real source of her failure lies within herself and her incapacity to listen to clear signals.

The ability to listen effectively ties back to my earlier discussion of empathy and dyssemia. As I have stated, empathy is an important social skill for a project professional to possess. A significant trait of empathetic people is that they have highly sensitive receptors that capture incoming signals. They are good listeners. If one's receptors are deactivated, however—as was the case with my student—then one lacks crucial incoming information.

Conclusions

It is impossible in the space of one chapter to deal thoroughly with the importance of social skills for the effective management of projects. The central point made here is that in the search for competent people to put on a project team, we must consciously seek men and women who possess more than book smarts. Although book smarts are necessary, they are not enough. Because project management is a social activity, when project team members must interact with managers, customers, and other team members, they need to possess good social skills.

Chapter Seven

Developing Business-Related Competence

Today's project professionals are expected to operate like good business men and women. Historically, project professionals were viewed as mere implementers. Project solutions would be developed with little or no input from the project team, then the team would be required to implement them. Team members generally had no cost accountability and certainly no profit-and-loss responsibilities. No one expected them to serve as marketers or to possess good customer relations skills. No one expected them to understand basic financial concepts such as present value, internal rate of return, and payback period. Seldom were they empowered to make independent decisions that had measurable business implications.

All that has changed. Today's competitive environment requires project professionals to operate like independent business men and women. They are expected to watch the bottom line and to be familiar with basic financial concepts. They are being told by their management that their job is to offer *solutions* to their customers. Consequently, they should know their customers' business and be able to talk their customers' language. On larger projects, project managers look very much like the presidents of small businesses, with responsibilities in the areas of finance, marketing, operations, and human resource management.

The emphasis on project professionals as business managers is reflected in the content of today's graduate degrees in project management. For example, at the University of Management and Technology, our newly established master's degree in project management is in effect a mini-MBA program with a strong slant toward the management of projects. Students take courses in finance, marketing, quantitative methods, operations, contracts and procurement, human resource management, and organizational behavior, in addition to project and program management courses.

In this chapter I approach business competence from two perspectives. The first perspective is what I call *business sense*. This is the practical insights that project professionals possess that enable them to make good business judgments. Today's effective project professionals are people who instinctively know which actions make good business sense and which do not. It is not a matter of having a rigorous business education. In fact, the majority of the most successful business people in history never studied business formally, and some notable successes—such as Benjamin Franklin, Aristotle Onassis, Ray Kroc, and Bill Gates—dropped out of school at a young age.

The second perspective is what I call *business knowledge*. This is the specialized business-focused knowledge that project professionals possess in areas such as finance, accounting, and marketing. Unlike business sense, business knowledge is acquired through conscious study.

Business Sense in Project Professionals

Some people possess intuitive understanding of what makes good business sense and what does not. Without ever having studied business formally, they have a talent for formulating problems in business terms. They visualize the consequences of different courses of action. They automatically assess the benefits against the costs of a decision. They recognize the importance of customers to the business and act accordingly. They have a little voice inside their head that warns them when things just don't look right, and they listen to that voice.

The value of good business sense is illustrated in the following case study, which illustrates two approaches to dealing with an unexpected problem. The first approach is taken by an individual lacking good business sense and the second by an individual who possesses it. The reader of this case study should recognize that the person making a good business decision is able to make good judgments without any specialized business knowledge.

Case Study: The Performance Effectiveness Society

The Performance Effectiveness Society is a professional society that focuses on implementing processes that improve the productivity of organizations. The society is sixteen years old and has witnessed a steady growth in its membership. At the time of its fifteenth anniversary it had more than twenty thousand members.

A major source of income for the society is skills-development workshops held during its annual meeting. The most successful workshop is entitled Assessing Effectiveness. Participants in the workshop pay $400 to attend a one-day session. Attendance at the workshop has grown steadily, and at the last offering 150 participants attended. This generated $60,000 in gross income to the society. Workshop expenses amounted to $6,000, so the net revenue associated with the workshop was $54,000.

The sixteenth annual meeting of the society is being held in Kansas City. Unfortunately, the hotel accommodations do not allow for holding classes of more than 70 people. The meeting organizers are shocked to learn about this restriction. They talk to the hotel management about acquiring space that can accommodate at least 150 people (the anticipated attendance at the Assessing Effectiveness workshop) but are told that the hotel is fully booked and the desired space is not available.

SCENARIO A: LET'S LIVE WITH THE LIMITATIONS

Marsha Smith is the workshop organizer. When she learns of the space limitations for workshops, she is upset because she knows that some society members will be disappointed that they cannot attend the popular Assessing Effectiveness workshop. She first contacts the hotel sales and catering manager to see if more spacious accommodations can be found. When this does not lead to the desired results, she contacts the general manager of the hotel, but even here she discovers that there is no way the hotel can help her resolve the problem. Consequently, she instructs the workshop registrar to inform applicants for the Assessing Effectiveness workshop that the workshop will be closed once seventy people have registered to attend it. Marsha never works out the revenue implications of this decision. Had she done so, she would have learned that the Performance Effectiveness Society will lose about $32,000 of income because of the space shortage (the lost income associated with 80 people at $400 per person).

SCENARIO B: THE LIMITATIONS ARE UNACCEPTABLE

Marsha Smith learns that the hotel is unable to provide her with the space she needs to hold a workshop for at least 150 participants. This upsets her because she knows that a number of society members will be disappointed that they cannot attend the popular Assessing Effectiveness workshop. She also recognizes that the hotel's space limitations will have a major negative impact on revenue generation. She determines that the revenue loss is likely to be $32,000. She checks with the hotel's general manager to see whether the space limitation is immutable and learns that it is. After making some inquiries, she discovers that a local university located one mile from the hotel has an auditorium that can easily accommodate an audience of 400 people. The cost of renting the auditorium is $2,000 per day. The obvious problem she now faces is how to get participants to the university auditorium. She contacts a local bus rental company and is told that she can rent a fifty-five-passenger bus for a day for $700 (including use of a driver). She enters into a contract with both the university and the bus company to provide the services the workshop needs. Although the additional expenses (the cost of renting the auditorium, renting a bus, and odds and ends) are $3,700, the increase in net revenue associated with the use of the auditorium is $28,300 ($32,000 in seminar fees minus the $3,700 in expenses).

Whom would you rather have working on your projects: the Marsha Smith of scenario A or the Marsha Smith of scenario B? Both Marsha A and Marsha B are dedicated, hardworking people. Marsha A followed up on the problem of space shortage by contacting the hotel's sales and catering staff as well as the general manager. She attempted to remedy the problem but found that there was nothing the hotel could do to help the society. In the end she decided to live with the problem and regretted the inconvenience this would cause the society's members.

Marsha B, in contrast, formulated the problem in business terms. She reckoned that not only would the hotel's space limitations lead to customer unhappiness (that is, disappointed society members) but it would also have a major impact on revenue generation. By formulating the problem in business terms, Marsha B was able to develop a solution that led to both customer happiness and increased revenues to the society.

A Business-Sense Experiment

Just for fun, I carried out an experiment as I was writing this chapter. For two weeks I tabulated instances when I encountered situations in which ordinary people in ordinary jobs demonstrated both good and bad business sense. I recommend that this book's readers try this experiment themselves because it illustrates dramatically how frequently people must make business-based judgments that have implications for the success of their operations. Unfortunately, I suspect that most of the experiments will show that a majority of people lack good business sense.

Item A: A Case of Good Sense

For one week I made daily visits to a building with a large foyer. My destination was an office on the mezzanine level, which could only be reached by means of a stairway or escalator. On the first day I noted that both the up and down escalators were under repair and nonfunctioning. I therefore had to climb the stairs to get to the mezzanine. Two technicians worked busily on the escalators and on the third day they prepared to reassemble them so they could function properly. I chatted with the technicians for a few moments about the mechanical features of escalators, then asked them when they would be finished with their work.

"It will take two days to reassemble the escalators," responded the chief technician. "We'll spend one day working on each."

"In what order will you reassemble them?" I asked.

"We'll work on the up escalator first," the technician answered.

I decided to press him for a more detailed response and asked, "Why the up escalator first?"

The technician looked at me as if I were feebleminded. Then he said, "Obviously it's harder to walk up the stairs than to walk down them. It doesn't make sense to start with the down escalator since that won't be a convenience to anybody. If we repair the up escalator first, this building's occupants will be convenienced more rapidly."

I gave the technicians an A for good, customer-focused business sense. I would like to have people like them on my project teams.

Item B: A Case of Bad Sense

A client organization invited me to speak to its senior managers about project management professionalism. I agreed to meet with them. The manager who issued the invitation told me to contact his secretary the next day to get detailed information on the location of the site where I would make my presentation. When I called the secretary she was cheerful and helpful. She told me she had the instructions on reaching the site written on a piece of paper that she could send to me.

"Could you fax it to me?" I asked.

"No problem," she answered. "My fax machine is about five feet away from me."

I gave her my fax number, thanked her for her help, and then went about my business.

First thing the next day an overnight courier came to my office with an envelope. When I opened it I found a one-page sheet of paper with directions on how to reach my client's facility. On the outside of the envelope I noted that the charge for overnight delivery was $9.00. Instead of faxing me the page (which would have cost about ten cents), the secretary had incurred a notable expense to send it via courier.

I gave the secretary a B plus for good cheer on the telephone, but an F for an absence of cost consciousness. Despite her sunny disposition, I would be reluctant to have her on my project teams because she appears to lack common sense.

Item C: A Case of Bad Sense

Earlier this year I was informed in a letter from my bank that a large check I had deposited had been rejected by the bank because it lacked microcoding at the bottom. In the ensuing three months I learned that my bank had lost the check, that the money had nonetheless been withdrawn from the account of my client (a Korean company), and that the local branch manager of my bank expected me to straighten out the problem with the Korean bank that had issued the check.

When it became obvious that the branch manager did not intend to help me recover the money that her branch had lost, I attempted to talk to the regional bank manager. When I contacted his office, his secretary said she would have the "right" person call me back to help me out. The right person turned out to be a customer service representative who admitted that she knew nothing about the banking process. She suggested that I try to reach another senior executive. When I contacted this person's office, the secretary forwarded my call to another customer service representative who, like the first one, informed me that she lacked the banking knowledge to deal with the problem. After repeated attempts I was unable to talk to any senior executive because of the defensive actions of secretaries who were intent on protecting their bosses from pesky customers. I was finally able to deal with a senior manager after I initiated legal action against the bank. This occurred during the two weeks of my experiment.

I gave the bank branch manager and the secretaries I spoke with F's for their disregard for their customers. I gave the customer service representatives D's because despite their outpouring of sympathy for my plight they did nothing to resolve the problem. I gave the senior management of the bank (one of the three largest banks in the United States) an F for running an organization that was incompetent and hostile to customers. I would not want to have any of these people working on my project teams.

Item D: A Case of Bad Sense

The afternoon before I was scheduled to meet some executives in a government agency, I encountered an emergency that would force me to be late to the meeting. I telephoned my contact at the agency and got his voice mail, which requested that I leave a message or dial a number to talk to an operator. I left a message for my contact and also tried to get ahold of the operator. I called several times but the operator never answered. I became desperate to talk to a human being to make sure my message would get through, so I called my contact's old phone number, hoping there would be someone there who could help me.

"Planning section," a voice answered.

I felt a sense of relief to hear a human voice. I explained my situation to the voice. He answered that he couldn't help me because my contact, whom he knew quite well, worked in a different department than he did. I told him I realized that but I hoped he could help me connect with someone, anyone, in the other department.

"What you should do is call the operator," he advised, sounding a bit testy.

"I've called the operator several times but no one answers the phone," I replied.

"Well, there's nothing I can do for you."

"Isn't your office just a couple of doors down the hall from the other department? Couldn't you walk down there to see if there's anybody I can talk to?"

"I'm afraid I can't," he said coldly. "Your best bet is to keep trying to get the operator." He then said he was busy and hung up.

I gave the voice an F for his sorry-it's-not-my-job attitude. I certainly would not want this character working on my project teams.

Item E: A Case of Good Sense

I bumped into a colleague in the hallway who was breathing heavily and sweating profusely.

"Have you been jogging?" I asked jokingly.

"Not quite. About a half hour ago I was sitting in my office when I received a phone call from a furniture delivery outfit. A dispatcher asked me if I would meet with their delivery team over at the new media center to receive some expensive cabinets that will house new multimedia equipment. I told him he must have a wrong number because I am a professor and have nothing at all to do with the media center.

"The dispatcher grew alarmed and said it was crucial for a representative of the university to sign for the equipment and assure the sender that it had arrived undamaged. I told the dispatcher not to worry, that I would run over to the media center to handle things. I had to ask the dispatcher for the center's address because I didn't even know where it's located.

"When I arrived at the center, the door was locked, so I located campus security and had them open it. When the equipment arrived I inspected it, found no damage, and signed for it. I locked the center door to make sure the cabinets were safe. I ran back here from the center because I don't want to miss my student office hours.

"By the way, do you have any idea who runs the center? I'd like to contact someone affiliated with the center to let them know their cabinets have arrived."

I gave my colleague an A for conscientiousness and a strong sense of responsibility. Although the delivery of the cabinets had nothing to do with her, she made it her problem. I'd certainly like to have her work on my project teams.

The individual decisions and actions of an organization's workforce have measurable business impacts. Consistently wise decisions and actions, as in items A and E, lead to increased customer satisfaction, cost savings, and improved efficiency and effectiveness. Consistently poor decisions and actions, as in Items B, C, and D, lead to customer unhappiness, ineffectiveness, and a loss of business.

These examples represent one half of the pertinent experiences I encountered in my two-week experiment. There is nothing unusual about any of them. During the course of a typical day, we all encounter such experiences—in checkout lines, in reconciling billing discrepancies, in calling the county tax hotline, and in ordering a meal at a restaurant. Often these experiences lead to frustration. Our expectations are that the problems we encounter in such experiences are inevitable and natural.

The fact is that there is nothing inevitable about most of the snafus we encounter in our daily lives and the inefficiencies we experience in the work world. This is an important lesson learned from the quality movement. Not long ago, customers expected the manufactured products they acquired to be bug ridden. The application of quality management principles, however, over the past four decades has shown that manufacturing errors can be largely eliminated. Motorola, for example, espouses the six-sigma principle, which tolerates only 3.4 mistakes per million items.

Although a number of elements contribute to the high quality of manufactured products, a key element is the *absolute commitment* of everyone in the organization to produce high-quality goods. This is captured in J. M. Juran's concept of "fitness for use" (1988, p. 5). This principle asks workers to see the next person on the assembly line as their customer. As a widget passes before them on the line, the workers should ask themselves, "Is this widget fit to be used by my customer, the next person on the assembly line?" If it is not, they should remedy whatever problem they encounter.

Ideally, all employees in an organization are committed to serving their customers and their organization well. The term *commitment* implies more than the *will* to do a good job. It also implies the *capability* to operate effectively. The project worker with good business sense possesses both the will and the capacity to operate effectively.

Key Traits of People with Good Business Sense

Business sense is an amorphous construct. Most people would be hard put to define it precisely. They would say, "I know it when I see it, but beyond that I can't really define it."

Like other people, I do not know how to define the concept precisely. I feel comfortable, however, in suggesting a few broad principles of what constitutes good business sense.

People with good business sense have the following general traits:

- *They can formulate issues in a business context.* They recognize that their decisions can have an impact on the organization's financial health and reputation. Thus, in making decisions, they think through the business implications. To sustain a sound business perspective, they maintain an air of detached impartiality. They do not see the issues they confront in a personal or political context. For example, they will not snub a customer simply because they do not like his attitude; rather, they view customers as a source of their organization's strength and future survival and treat them accordingly.
- *They have an intuitive grasp of benefit-cost trade-offs.* I recently asked the president of a small business which trait is most important to her in hiring new employees. She answered, "They have to be able to weigh the benefits of their actions against the costs." She went on to explain that this is a feature she seeks in all of her employees, not just her managers. For example, she described a proposal writer who decided he would learn how to use a new desktop publishing package to create graphics for a proposal he was working on. The problem was he was spending hours teaching himself new software skills when he should have been cranking out a proposal that had a pressing deadline. He did not understand that whatever benefits he would derive from learning the new software package would not offset the costs he would incur by missing a proposal deadline.
- *They don't see themselves as bureaucrats and are capable of pursuing out-of-the-box thinking.* Bureaucratic thinking is the antithesis of good business sense. The methods and procedures that drive bureaucracies are designed to serve as substitutes for independent,

intelligent thinking. This is not necessarily bad. For example, following prescribed methods and procedures is crucial in carrying out routine operations. We do not want order processors to change ordering procedures on a whim because they believe their procedures are better than existing procedures. Such actions would create chaos. A key characteristic of projects, however, is that they often do not entail routine activity. Decision makers on projects recognize that they often have to think "out of the box" if they are to offer good solutions to the ever-changing challenges they face.

- *They are capable of articulating their viewpoints.* People with good business sense are able to articulate their views clearly. This capacity for articulation serves at least two functions. First, it enables them to demonstrate that they have a good understanding of the circumstances they face. Fuzzy thinkers cannot articulate their viewpoints effectively. Second, people with well-articulated views can communicate those views to other people, thereby gaining their support.

- *They have a strong sense of personal accountability.* People with good business sense possess a strong sense of personal accountability. When they make decisions, they recognize that these decisions have consequences. They are willing to live with the consequences. This sense of personal accountability manifests itself when individuals make purchasing decisions as if they were spending their own money. It is also seen when individuals refuse to goof off on the job. People who waste time on the job and spend the organization's money lavishly lack a sense of personal accountability and do not add value to the organization's business. Tom Peters (1994) believes that this sense of personal accountability is one of the most significant traits of an effective worker when he suggests that the best workers are those who make decisions as if they were independent entrepreneurs.

Business Knowledge in Project Professionals

The expectation today is that competent project professionals possess basic business skills. But what *specific* business knowledge should the competent project professional possess? There is no clear-cut answer to this question. The best answer, in my opinion, is *more is better.* For example, it is clear to me that on a multiyear project the project professional who is able to compute the present value of cash outflows and inflows has a better understanding of financial issues on the project than the professional who is ignorant of basic finance. Similarly, the project professional who understands contracting and procurement specifics is better positioned to deal with outsourcing issues than the professional who does not.

Project professionals need business knowledge for another reason as well. They need it to deal more effectively with their customers and their management. This is a central point emphasized by Mack Hanon in his seminal work *Consultative Selling* (1985). Hanon was one the first business consultants to emphasize that the organization's job is not to sell customers goods per se; rather, it is to sell them *solutions*. One of the best ways of selling solutions is to show how a given solution makes good business sense (such as it increases profitability). It is difficult to make a convincing business argument supporting a given solution if one does not have rudimentary knowledge of such things as computing profit, developing cash flow statements, calculating discounted cash flows, and understanding market share.

Everything I have said here about selling solutions to customers also applies to gaining support from one's own management. Chances are that one's managers' performance is assessed against some clearly defined financial and marketing targets. If teams want support from managers in order to acquire more people, new equipment, and more training, they need to make a case for how their requests make good business sense and will help managers achieve their business targets.

Perhaps the best way to identify the basic business knowledge that project professionals should possess is to outline the course requirements of a typical MBA student, because MBA degrees epitomize the education community's vision of the needed business knowledge of the best-educated businesspeople. MBA graduates are expected to possess general business insights that can be applied across a broad range of business activity. Following is an outline of the core course requirements of a typical MBA program:

- *Introduction to financial accounting.* This course provides a rudimentary understanding of basic accounting concepts and tools, such as balance sheets, income statements, cash flow statements, and capital budgeting tools (present value, internal rate of return, and payback period analysis). Beyond this, the diligent MBA student can take a course on managerial accounting, which focuses on the use of accounting for business decision making.

- *Introduction to finance.* Such a course provides a rudimentary understanding of the role of finance in business operations. The focus is on topics such as sources of capital, how the financial function is carried out in organizations, understanding the role of financial risk in making investment decisions, and appreciating how different financial tools can be employed to improve financial performance.

- *Organizational behavior and development.* This course offers a study of basic organizational issues, including the role of people in business, structural factors, political factors, and "symbolic" factors (Bolman and Deal, 1997). Specific treatment is given to team building and managing conflict. Beyond this, MBA programs also offer a number of courses on human resource management, labor relations, and organizational design.

- *Quantitative methods in decision making.* This course teaches how to use quantitative tools for decision-making purposes, often including an introduction to linear programming, goal programming, queuing theory, and related decision-making techniques. The course also addresses topics in statistics, such as linear regression, analysis of variance, and Monte Carlo simulation.

- *Information systems.* The course offers an overview of the role of computers in business. Practical insights are offered into how computer systems operate, the role of database systems, the role of information systems, the use of spreadsheets, and desktop publishing.

- *Introduction to marketing.* This course reviews the "four P's" of marketing: product, price, promotion, and place. It explicates various marketing activities, such as market research and advertising, and introduces customer behavior.

- *Introduction to operations.* This course provides an overview of manufacturing. It deals with a wide variety of manufacturing-related topics, such as maintaining inventory, estimating manufacturing capacity, and quality control.

- *Social and legal environment of business.* This course presents insights into a broad array of business law topics, from contracting to understanding different forms of business to dealing with regulations. In addition, it reviews contemporary social issues, including business responsibility in the areas of the environment, poverty, and education.

- *Business ethics.* This course examines ethical and unethical behavior found in business. Topics include dealing honestly with employees, identifying conflicts of interest, and eschewing criminal activities.
- *International dimensions of business.* This course recognizes the growing importance of global business transactions. It gives students an overview of the principles of international trade, describes how multinationals operate, and introduces cross-cultural affairs.

These courses constitute the core curriculum of a typical MBA program. Students are also expected to develop specialized knowledge in advanced-level courses. For example, financial majors, organizational behavior majors, and marketing majors may be required to take three or four advanced courses in their field beyond the courses listed in the core.

The purpose of examining the curriculum of a typical MBA program is not to encourage project professionals to get an MBA. It is simply an attempt to identify the standard view of what the well-educated business person should know. Individual project professionals might want to assess their business knowledge against the knowledge promoted in an MBA curriculum to determine whether they have knowledge gaps that they should fill.

Conclusions

As stated at the outset of this chapter, project professionals today are expected to have solid business skills. Gone are the days when they were mere implementers of other people's solutions.

In this chapter I have pointed out that business skills have two components: good business sense and good business knowledge. In assessing the capabilities of project workers, we need to determine whether they have adequate portions of both.

It is relatively easy to measure competencies associated with basic business knowledge. For instance, students can be shown a cash flow and asked to compute its present value assuming a 15 percent cost of capital; they can be asked to contrast the relative merits of decentralized versus centralized computing operations;

or they can be asked to explain Maslow's hierarchy of needs. These types of questions have demonstrably correct and incorrect answers. One either knows or does not know the correct answer.

It is clearly more difficult to assess competencies associated with good business sense. How does one measure whether prospective project workers make decisions as if they were spending their own money? How does one identify whether they are sensitive to customers' needs and wants? How does one determine whether they are able to balance benefits against costs in an effective fashion?

Although it is difficult to measure the business-sense competencies of project workers, it is nonetheless important that these competencies be addressed. For the most part, they will be assessed by subjective means. Important questions to be answered include, Do prospective workers have a track record of working in jobs that require some measure of business-related decision making? If so, what kind of business issues have these people faced? Have they demonstrated sensitivity to costs? Have they interacted effectively with customers? Have they demonstrated the capacity to carry out their work in a consistent, reliable fashion?

Answers to these and other questions can be gleaned by interviewing previous supervisors and customers. It may even be appropriate to talk to vendors who worked with the prospective project workers in the past.

A grasp of prospective project workers' business sense can also be gained by direct interviews with them. If they come from the technical ranks, do they show any inclination to deal with the outside world? Do they understand current events that are routinely reported in the news? Do they show any entrepreneurial flair?

Organizations that are seriously interested in measuring business-sense competencies may even be able to establish crude competency tests. One approach would be to create simple scenarios and present them to prospective workers. For example, prospective workers could be asked to read a scenario such as the one about the Performance Effectiveness Society offered early in this chapter and asked to identify what courses of action are open to the protagonists. It is important that the chosen scenarios be relevant to the job that the proposed worker will carry out.

After all is said and done, we must be humble in our opinion of our capacity to identify competent workers. History is filled with examples of the inability of people to assess who is capable of carrying out a job and who is not. One of the most dramatic exemplars of this point was Ulysses S. Grant. Grant was a middling student at West Point, where he graduated in the bottom half of his class. During the Mexican War he showed himself to be a capable commander. Personal problems, however, including alcoholism, caused him to resign from the army and try his hand in the private sector. He became a farmer, and failed at this enterprise. He then joined his father's leather-tanning operation, where he was employed at the outbreak of the Civil War. Owing to his military background, he was able to enlist in the Union Army as a colonel. Throughout the war he demonstrated consistent military capability. His genius lay in his understanding of the connection between military action and economic forces. He employed the economic might of the North to crush the agrarian South. To fully appreciate his achievement, one has to recall that Lincoln went through a string of superficially "brilliant" commanders who in the field proved to be incompetent before finally settling on the rather plebeian Grant.

During the war, Grant showed himself to be a military genius who was able to manage a complex enterprise. One would imagine that such a track record would show him to be an effective manager capable of managing any complex undertaking—but one would be wrong. After the war, Grant was elected president of the United States. Regrettably, his military experience did not prepare him to deal with the rough and tumble of civilian political life. His administration is often cited as the single most corrupt administration in the history of the American presidency. As a general, Grant was a genius. As a president, he was an utter failure.

The case of Ulysses S. Grant illustrates the pitfalls of predicting competence on the basis of an individual's track record. Grant's performance at West Point showed him to be a below-average military student. His performance during the Mexican Wars was impressive. His life as a civilian after the Mexican Wars puts him in the ranks of business failures. Although the leadership opportunities afforded him during the Civil War highlighted his capacity to manage complexity, his military experience was unfortunately not a good predictor of his competence in the civilian sector; he turned out to be one of the worst presidents in American history.

Chapter Eight

Assessing Individual Competence

This chapter offers a diagnostic tool to help project professionals identify their own levels of knowledge-based project management competence. The tool is a multiple-choice examination that raises questions in assorted knowledge areas. It conforms roughly to the approach taken by the Project Management Institute in implementing its project management certification process.

The diagnostic tool comprises eight sections, each corresponding to one of the eight functional knowledge areas contained in the institute's *Guide to the Project Management Body of Knowledge* (Duncan, 1996): scope management, time management, cost management, human resource management, risk management, quality management, procurement management, and communication management. You should take the whole exam in one sitting within a one-hundred-minute period. Correct answers are listed at the end of the exam. To "pass" the exam, you should get at least seven correct answers per section. If you score fewer than seven correct answers in a section, this indicates some "softness" in your grasp of the material in the targeted knowledge area.

Project Management Competence Diagnostic Examination

Time Management

1. Given the following data on Task A, what is the task's expected duration? Shortest duration = 5 days, longest

duration = 9 days, most frequent duration = 6 days, standard deviation = 0.67 days, number of task components = 3.
a. 5⅔ days
b. 6½ days
c. 6⅓ days
d. 7⅓ days
e. 6⅔ days

2. Tasks B and D, both of which lie on the critical path, take 4 and 6 days, respectively, to carry out. Task E, which is carried out parallel to the other two tasks, has 2 days of slack. How much slack do Tasks B and D together have?
   a. 0 days
   b. 1 day
   c. 2 days
   d. 3 days
   e. 4 days

3. Which of the following is an important component of "crashing" a schedule?
   a. Identifying key costs elements of the WBS
   b. Crashing tasks that lie on the critical path
   c. Removing low-productivity players from the project team
   d. Conducting damage-control exercises
   e. Removing tasks whose perceived value is low

4. Which is not a strength of the Gantt chart approach to scheduling?
   a. It is simple to learn.
   b. It is simple to use.
   c. It enables team members to compare readily actual and planned performance.
   d. It is tied to a time line.
   e. It shows the interrelationships of tasks.

5. Given the following information, identify schedule variance: BCWP = 800, ACWP = 900, BCWS = 850, EAC = 125,000, CPI = 0.89.
   a. −50
   b. 50

    c. −100

    d. 100

    e. −150

6. Given the following information, identify what proportion of the targeted work has been performed: BCWP = 800, ACWP = 900, BCWS = 850, EAC = 125,000, CPI = 0.89.
   a. 0.83
   b. 0.94
   c. 0.62
   d. 1.06
   e. 1.12

7. What does fast-tracking entail?
   a. Employing high-performing workers on the project team
   b. Carrying out tasks parallel to the extent possible
   c. Adding resources to critical path tasks
   d. Adding resources to tasks whose marginal cost of performance is lowest
   e. Obtaining top management support to add additional resources to the project

8. What kind of reasoning does the following sequencing of tasks illustrate? *First conduct a survey of the land, then excavate.*
   a. Syllogistic reasoning
   b. Deductive reasoning
   c. Inductive reasoning
   d. Soft logic
   e. Hard logic

9. Five people working full-time over three days have undertaken how much work effort?
   a. 8 person-days
   b. 3 person-days
   c. 15 person-days
   d. 2 person-days
   e. 7 person-days

10. Task A (three-day effort) begins first thing Monday morning. Task A has a finish-to-finish link with Task B (two-day effort).

This finish-to-finish link has a two-day lag. When does Task B begin?
a. End of workday on Tuesday
b. Beginning of workday on Wednesday
c. Beginning of workday on Tuesday
d. Beginning of workday on Thursday
e. End of workday on Thursday

Cost Management

1. Bottom-up cost estimating entails
    a. Identifying costs of work packages and then rolling them up
    b. Using a mathematical cost model
    c. Using basic design-to-cost principles
    d. Employing simulation
    e. Identifying cost constants

2. A chart of accounts
    a. Lists costs on a per-task basis
    b. Enables cost estimators to calculate Estimate a Complete (EAC)
    c. Is instrumental in constructing an organizational break-down structure (OBS)
    d. Is a life-cycle cost-estimating tool
    e. Is a coding structure for reporting financial information on the general ledger

3. An S-curve portrays
    a. Anticipated costs for a particular point in time
    b. Anticipated cumulative costs for a particular point in time
    c. Project costs, with overhead costs factored out
    d. Project costs, with overhead and fringe-benefit costs factored out
    e. Anticipated operations and maintenance costs

4. A key feature of a life-cycle cost estimate is
    a. It is produced by a cost-estimation department.
    b. It must be reviewed and approved by the client.
    c. It must be produced using bottom-up cost estimates.

d. It includes operations and maintenance costs in addition to project costs.

e. It must make cost projections by adjusting for inflation.

5. Calculate cost variance given the following information: BCWP = 800, ACWP = 900, BCWS = 850, EAC = 125,000, and CPI = 0.89.
   a. −50
   b. 50
   c. −100
   d. 100
   e. −150

6. Forecast the final cost of a $100,000 project given the following information: BCWP = $800, ACWP = $900, BCWS = $850.
   a. $88,889
   b. $93,499
   c. $100,000
   d. $112,500
   e. $116,480

7. If you put $10 in the bank and it is compounded annually at a 10 percent rate, you will have $11.00, $12.10, and $13.31 in the bank at the beginning of years 2, 3, and 4, respectively. (Assumptions: there are no transaction costs, and principal and interest are left untouched in the account.) In making a cost estimate, you calculate that you will have a cost outlay of $250,000 at the beginning of year 4. Using the data supplied, what is the present value of that cost outlay?
   a. $332,750
   b. $187,829
   c. $227,227
   d. $250,000
   e. $206,612

8. Mary invested $1,000 in a project opportunity. At the end of the year the project was completed and she was given $1,100. In talking to her colleague Stan she learned that when she had made her investment, he also had invested $1,000 in an-

other project and had received $1,400 at the end of the project. What was the opportunity cost Mary encountered in investing the way she did?
a. $1,000
b. $1,100
c. $100
d. $300
e. $400

9. According to the law of diminishing returns, as you increase inputs into a process, output
   a. Decreases
   b. Remains constant
   c. Increases
   d. Decreases at an increasing rate
   e. Increases at a decreasing rate

10. Which of the following items represents direct costs?
    a. Staff salaries
    b. Office rent
    c. Fringe benefits
    d. Employee insurance
    e. Profit-sharing plan

Human Resource Management

1. A chart that shows who is supposed to do what is called a
   a. Resource histogram
   b. Resource loading chart
   c. Statement of work (SOW)
   d. Responsibility matrix
   e. Line-of-balance chart

2. Matrix management can create team-building problems because
   a. Top management authority is weakened.
   b. Project team members are borrowed resources.
   c. Budgetary authority is held by the accounting department.

    d. Project managers need to have a strong technical background.

    e. Team members operate in a chain-of-command structure.

3. As organizations face tremendous resource constraints, they increasingly acquire resources from outside the organization through a process called
    a. Outsourcing
    b. Winnowing
    c. Culling
    d. Reengineering
    e. Self-management

4. Who possesses the ultimate responsibility for project performance?
    a. Top management
    b. Middle management
    c. The functional manager
    d. The project manager
    e. The technicians

5. Which of the following is a trait typically associated with the smoothing approach to conflict resolution?
    a. Problems get resolved.
    b. Contentious issues are glossed over.
    c. Negotiations carried out to deal with conflict get stretched out.
    d. Attention focuses on identifying root causes of problems.
    e. It is based on win-lose thinking.

6. What is not a problem that project managers commonly encounter when they are involved in conducting performance appraisal reviews of project team members in a typical matrix organization?
    a. They may not be technically competent to assess the workers' efforts.
    b. They may be unaware of career objectives established for the workers.
    c. They may only see one facet of the workers' work lives.

   d. They aren't generally trained on how to carry out perfor-
      mance appraisals.

   e. They have a chance to see the workers' work firsthand.

7. The process of adjusting allocations of scheduled activities to
accommodate the availability of resources is called
   a. Smoothing
   b. Heuristics
   c. Concurrent engineering
   d. Logic analysis
   e. Resource leveling

8. The chief function of the resource loading chart (also called
the resource histogram) is to provide project staff with information on
   a. Resource costs associated with each task
   b. Number of resources required on the project over a given
      period
   c. Task assignments for each project worker over the life of
      the project
   d. Actual versus planned employment of individual resources
   e. A link between resource allocations and the work break-
      down structure

9. Motivating people by giving them responsibility and allowing
them to grow on the job is an example of
   a. Benign neglect
   b. Enlightened self-interest
   c. Employment of the managerial grid
   d. Self-actualization
   e. Theory X management

10. A key strength of the projectized structure to managing projects is
   a. It provides functional managers with more authority to
      manage their resources.
   b. It reduces fringe benefit costs associated with carrying out
      the project.
   c. It does not require the organization to engage in activity-
      based accounting practices.

    d. It gives project workers more flexibility in selecting job assignments.

    e. It gives project managers a measure of direct control over resources.

Risk Management

1. As the uncertainty associated with a set of tasks grows, project managers must be prepared to
   a. Accept that the proposed work will cost more than was planned.
   b. Reconcile themselves to inevitable losses.
   c. Accept more variance in the accuracy of cost and schedule estimates.
   d. Write very detailed project plans.
   e. Quantify the costs and benefits of the proposed activities.

2. When contrasting *risk* with *uncertainty*, the project team member is dealing with
   a. The opportunity for gain as well as for loss
   b. Knowledge of the probability of an event
   c. A quantitative measurement of stake
   d. A balance against reward
   e. A measure of economic loss

3. Which of the following is not an example of risk deflection (also called risk transfer)?
   a. Insurance
   b. Warranty
   c. Guarantee
   d. Contract
   e. Management reserve

4. Monte Carlo simulation is based on computing outcomes
   a. Iteratively, using estimates generated by a random number generator
   b. Using a PERT chart to model project schedules
   c. By gambling on certain predetermined patterns of activity
   d. By simulating anticipated reactions of opponents to given actions

e. By comparing them pairwise for different payoff possibilities

5. Assuming a beta distribution for the allocation of human resources to carry out a job, what is the mean number of people estimated if the least number of people who have traditionally done the job is thirteen, the largest number is seventeen, and the most typical number is fourteen?
    a. 14.0
    b. 14.7
    c. 14.3
    d. 14.5
    e. 15.0

6. Martha has invested $50,000 to carry out work on a contracted project. If she delivers a product on or before a scheduled delivery date, she will be paid $130,000 for her work. If she misses this delivery date, her work will be rejected and she will be paid nothing. The probability of meeting the delivery date is 80 percent. What is the expected monetary value associated with this project effort?
    a. $34,000
    b. $30,000
    c. $54,000
    d. $62,000
    e. Nothing, because she will forfeit her investment

7. An external source of risk facing a project team might be
    a. A technical problem arising from sloppy work
    b. A change in government regulations
    c. Miscommunication among team members
    d. Poor procedures for project tracking
    e. A computer breakdown

8. George and Martha are in charge of organizing a picnic on Sunday. On Saturday they call up the weather service and learn that there is a 30 percent chance of rain for Sunday. If it is raining, there is a 10 percent chance that enough people will show up for the picnic to go ahead with it. If it is sunny, there is an 80 percent chance that enough people will show

up for the picnic to go ahead with it. What is the probability that the picnic will be held?

a. .056
b. 0.59
c. 0.45
d. 0.41
e. 0.70

9. On a typical project, as it is being carried out over time,
    a. Risk goes up, stake goes up.
    b. Risk goes down, stake goes down.
    c. Risk goes up, stake goes down.
    d. Risk goes down, stake goes up.
    e. Risk and stake vary randomly.

10. Unknown unknowns are the most difficult risk events to manage. A key strategy for dealing with them is
    a. Pursuing a risk-avoidance strategy
    b. Doing nothing until bad things happen, because they are total surprises and there is not much that can be done
    c. Establishing management reserves
    d. Computing the probability of the unknown unknowns occurring and identifying their cost consequences
    e. Computing the probability of the unknown unknowns occurring and acting on the results of the analysis

Contract Management

1. A narrative description of work to be carried out on the project is called
    a. A statement of work (SOW)
    b. A job assignment
    c. The project baseline
    d. A chart of accounts
    e. The master plan

2. Value engineering is employed on projects when the "owner"
    a. Is not sure what the deliverable should look like
    b. Wants to encourage the contractor to save money and speed up work

    c. Has relatively low operating expenses

    d. Wants to increase his or her role in managing project activities

    e. Anticipates that requirements will shift and large amounts of change will occur on the project

3. Issuing a project tender to possible contractors is best done through

    a. A public relations firm

    b. A request for proposal (RFP)

    c. A statement of work (SOW)

    d. Negotiation of a best and final offer (BAFO)

    e. Use of advertising space in trade journals

4. On a cost-plus-fixed-fee (CPFF) contract, the estimated project costs are $100,000. The buyer and contractor negotiate a fee based on 10 percent of the estimated project costs. The project duration is ten months. The contract is actually completed in nine months. The fee paid to the contractor will be

    a. $9,000

    b. $10,000

    c. $11,000

    d. $9,100

    e. $20,000

5. If negotiators take a zero-sum game approach to negotiating a contract, they are taking a position that stands in contrast to

    a. Standard contracting regulations

    b. A corporate procurement policy

    c. A lose-win position

    d. A win-lose position

    e. A win-win position

6. As a project is being closed out, a common source of conflict arises in

    a. Determining the best use of the time of design personnel

    b. The buyer's and the contractor's making different interpretations of whether terms and conditions have been met

    c. Determining whether the cost-plus-award fee (CPAF) or

cost-plus-incentive fee (CPIF) contract structure is most
appropriate

   d. Identifying the primary causes of monthly variances on
the project

   e. Identifying who has primary responsibility for paying
closeout costs

7. When disputes arise in a project, the best way to deal with
them at the outset is to

   a. Initiate legal proceedings to resolve them through the ju-
dicial system.

   b. Take them before an arbitration board for resolution.

   c. See if they can be resolved amicably in the best interests
of all parties.

   d. Stop all work on the project until the disputes have been
resolved.

   e. Hold off dealing with them until the customer-acceptance
stage.

8. In contracting, target costs should be established in order to

   a. Identify the basis for computing incentive fee payments.

   b. Provide the basis for computing cost and schedule
variances.

   c. Ensure that the contractor operates in accordance with
the terms and conditions of the contract.

   d. Provide the basis for computing the profitability of the
project.

   e. Provide the basis for making preliminary cost estimates.

9. The procurement management plan

   a. Focuses on identifying qualified vendors who will be encouraged to bid on solicitations

   b. Ties procurement activity to project activity by identifying
procurement actions in the PERT/CPM chart

   c. Focuses on providing a detailed accounting of prices that
can be paid for a set of predetermined products

   d. Is basically concerned with providing checklists to assist
the organization's contract managers through the
customer-acceptance process

    e. Describes how the procurement process (from solicitation planning through contract closeout) will be managed

10. Owners issue a back charge when
    a. The work they receive from the contractor is deficient and they incur expenses to make the deliverable function properly.
    b. Their customers want additional work performed beyond the work described in the original SOW.
    c. They can offer their contractors awards for performing the job earlier and at a lower cost than planned.
    d. Contract-based adjustments for inflation are insufficient to cover the true increase in inflation.
    e. Their suppliers supply more than they ordered.

Communication Management

1. To make sure that requirements are communicated effectively, it is wise to
    a. Get feedback from the recipient of the requirements, indicating that he or she understands them.
    b. Specify the requirements in detailed technical terms.
    c. Have the requirements developed by technical experts.
    d. Both a and b.
    e. Both b and c.

2. George is providing some information to Martha. Which of the following is not an example of nonverbal communication on Martha's part?
    a. When given some news, she emits a groan.
    b. She begins fidgeting.
    c. She gets upset and tells George that he is wrong in his assertions.
    d. She gets upset and turns red.
    e. She smiles as George is talking.

3. If Martha wants to make an important point and catch George's attention, she can express the urgency of her point most effectively by

   a. Sending him an e-mail message

   b. Sending him a detailed memorandum, laying out her position

   c. Asking a friend of George's to intervene in communicating her concerns

   d. Encountering George directly and voicing her viewpoint strongly, face-to-face

   e. Expressing her point through innuendo

4. Research and experience show that informal modes of communication
   a. Are not effective in conveying information
   b. Destroy team cohesiveness because they go outside established communication channels
   c. Lack credibility
   d. Are often more effective in conveying information than formal modes of communication
   e. Are difficult to employ

5. A coach issues a requirement to a member of his or her swimming team. Which of the following statements of this requirement is expressed most effectively?
   a. Using the freestyle stroke, swim four laps of the twenty-five-meter pool fast enough to beat your opponents in the next swim meet.
   b. Using the freestyle stroke, swim four laps of the twenty-five-meter pool in one minute or less by the time of your next swim meet.
   c. Using whatever stroke you believe is appropriate, swim four laps of the twenty-five-meter pool fast enough to beat your opponents in the next swim meet.
   d. Using the freestyle stroke, swim one hundred meters fast enough to beat your opponents in the next swim meet.
   e. Using the freestyle stroke, swim one hundred meters in one minute or less by the time of your next swim meet.

6. On large projects, detailed documentation
   a. Should be avoided to the extent possible because it adds to bureaucracy and project costs

b. Has costs that typically lie in the 10 to 15 percent range
c. Is needed to keep track of what is happening
d. Can be avoided by employing a skunk-works approach to project execution
e. Both a and d

7. Which of the following actions is typically not carried out during a kickoff meeting?
   a. Detailed assignments are given for carrying out project tasks.
   b. The project players are introduced.
   c. The project charter is presented.
   d. A higher-level manager makes a presentation expressing the significance of the project effort.
   e. Key milestones are identified.

8. Which of the following is not generally viewed as a barrier to communication?
   a. The "signal" is lost in the "noise."
   b. Encoding and decoding mechanisms are out of sync.
   c. Feedback is not offered.
   d. The sender and receiver of information are technical people.
   e. The receiver of information is known to explode in anger when receiving bad news.

9. As team size increases arithmetically (that is, uniformly), the number of communication channels that potentially must be managed
   a. Increases linearly
   b. Remains constant until the project reaches a critical size, then grows exponentially
   c. Actually decreases, confirming the principle of diminishing marginal returns
   d. Is unaffected
   e. Increases exponentially

10. On international projects, there is obviously tremendous opportunity for miscommunication. Which of the following is not likely to create miscommunication on international projects?

a. Project team members speaking different languages
b. Project team members operating from different cultural frameworks
c. Fluctuating exchange rates leading to unreliable cost estimates
d. Project team members operating in different time zones
e. The project environments of the different team players operating under different sets of national regulations

Scope Management

1. A work package is
   a. The lowest level of a work breakdown structure
   b. The level of the WBS where cost data are collected
   c. Made up of multiple costs accounts
   d. Both a and b
   e. Both b and c

2. What is not a feature of the product-oriented WBS?
   a. It is a good cost-estimating tool.
   b. It lends itself to contracting out subcomponents of the product.
   c. It focuses on the tangible aspects of the product being produced.
   d. It focuses on what should be produced rather than on how it should be produced.
   e. It shows how tasks are interconnected.

3. When taking a life-cycle perspective on a project,
   a. Look at the present value of cash flows.
   b. Compute internal rate of return.
   c. Look at operations and maintenance activities in addition to project activities.
   d. Examine sunk costs systematically during different reporting periods.
   e. Review a period equal to the depreciation period for the product being produced by the project.

4. A document that formally recognizes the existence of a project and identifies the project's authority is called

    a. A request for proposal (RFP)
    b. An invitation for bid (IFB)
    c. A statement of work (SOW)
    d. A preliminary plan
    e. A project charter

5. Details of efforts associated with a WBS element are contained in
    a. A WBS dictionary
    b. The organizational breakdown structure (OBS)
    c. The proposal
    d. The project postmortem
    e. The statement of work (SOW)

6. The principal responsibility of a change control board (CCB) is to
    a. Offer guidance on the technical merits of change requests.
    b. Suggest better ways in which the project team can carry out its efforts.
    c. Offer inputs into calculating the cost of scope changes.
    d. Review the managerial implications of change requests (that is, impacts on time, budget, and quality).
    e. Help project staff fill out change request forms.

7. In change management processes, the concept of traceability refers to
    a. Identifying who has responsibility to grant change requests
    b. Debugging problems that arise as they arise
    c. Tracking the evolution of a product by means of a numbering system
    d. Locating the source of project authority by reviewing the project charter
    e. Presenting change requests to a change control board

8. In MBO, what is (are) the characteristic(s) of a well-formulated objective?
    a. It is realistic.
    b. It is unambiguous.

    c. It is closely tied to the organization's profit and loss statements.

    d. Both a and b.

    e. Both b and c.

9. A benefit-cost ratio value of 2.35 indicates that

    a. Each unit of a good produced will generate a loss of $2.35.

    b. Each unit of a good produced will generate a profit of $1.35.

    c. For each dollar invested in the project, revenue of $2.35 will be generated.

    d. For each dollar invested in the project, $2.35 should be set aside to cover contingencies.

    e. There is a high chance that project profit will lie within 2.35 standard deviations of the expected mean.

10. Which of the following is not a strength of the Murder Board approach to selecting new projects?

    a. The project champion will be well prepared in making his or her presentation.

    b. Problems inherent in the project will be identified at the earliest stage possible.

    c. The cross-functional board members can contribute insights in a wide range of areas, thereby strengthening the project proposal.

    d. Projects that successfully make it through the review will have strong backing within the organization.

    e. The process encourages people to bring forth highly innovative, untested ideas.

Quality Management

1. Variances that occur outside the upper and lower control limits

    a. Are natural and should be accepted

    b. Should be brought to the attention of higher levels of management for appropriate action

    c. Are reflections of high-quality production

d. Represent measurement error
e. Occur only one out of twenty times

2. The process of evaluating overall project performance on a regular basis to provide confidence that the project satisfies relevant quality standards is called
   a. Quality assurance
   b. Quality control
   c. Variance analysis
   d. Management by exception
   e. Quality limits

3. Ultimately, quality is concerned with
   a. Delivering goods on time
   b. Delivering goods within budget
   c. Delivering goods according to specifications
   d. Delivering goods on time, within budget, and according to specifications
   e. Achieving customer satisfaction

4. ISO 9000 registration ensures that an organization
   a. Produces high-quality products
   b. Has had its products tested to meet the highest standards
   c. Can conduct business in North America
   d. Has had its processes reviewed and carries out its quality-related activities in a consistent way
   e. Is perceived to produce high-quality goods

5. Careful inspection of goods and services produced
   a. Is the most effective way to ensure the delivery of quality products
   b. Requires the physical destruction of the goods being inspected
   c. Needs to be carried out only from time to time
   d. Should be carried out on the first 10 percent of delivered goods
   e. Is not as effective a way to ensure quality as building quality into processes

6. Pareto's rule suggests that
   a. Eighty percent of quality problems are attributable to 20 percent of possible problem sources.
   b. The greater the volume of goods that are produced, the lower will be the unit costs of production.
   c. Efficiency decreases after a certain point in the production of goods and services.
   d. Projects should no longer receive project support when costs exceed benefits.
   e. Deficiencies should exist out of the six-sigma range.

7. In most cases, the cost of implementing quality programs
   a. Will be very expensive
   b. Will be zero
   c. Will be repaid quickly through reduced expenses of rework
   d. Should be categorized as a direct expense
   e. Need not be taken into account when computing project profitability

8. Kaisen is
   a. A fundamental operation carried out by keiretsu
   b. A cost minimization, profit maximization strategy
   c. Continuous quality improvement
   d. Employment of fishbone diagrams to find cause-and-effect relations
   e. Maintenance of quality by using the six-sigma standard

9. The zero defects concept
   a. Has zero tolerance for defects
   b. Attempts to define quality according to the six-sigma range
   c. Aspires to reduce defects to the smallest possible number through a process of continuous improvement
   d. Requires that workers' bonuses be tied to the number of defects associated with their work (that is, fewer defects, higher bonuses)
   e. Is an integral part of quality circle activity

10. Research shows that the vast majority of quality problems
  a. Are accounted for by the poor work habits of project workers
  b. Can be reduced cost-effectively by increased inspection
  c. Lie outside the control of workers and are basically tied to management responsibility
  d. Result because insufficient resources are provided to quality assurance departments
  e. Are caused by fickle customer expectations

Scoring Sheet

Time Management	Cost Management	Human Resources Management	Risk Management
1. c	1. a	1. d	1. c
2. a	2. e	2. b	2. b
3. b	3. b	3. a	3. e
4. e	4. d	4. d	4. a
5. a	5. c	5. b	5. c
6. b	6. d	6. e	6. c
7. b	7. b	7. e	7. b
8. e	8. d	8. b	8. b
9. c	9. e	9. d	9. d
10. d	10. a	10. e	10. c

Contract Management	Communication Management	Scope Management	Quality Management
1. a	1. a	1. d	1. b
2. b	2. c	2. e	2. a
3. b	3. d	3. c	3. e
4. b	4. d	4. e	4. d
5. e	5. b	5. a	5. e
6. b	6. c	6. d	6. a
7. c	7. a	7. c	7. c
8. a	8. d	8. d	8. c
9. e	9. e	9. c	9. c
10. a	10. c	10. e	10. c

Part Three

The Competent Project Team

Chapter Nine

Project Team Competence

The basic work unit of projects is the team. Whether the project entails building a factory, carrying out basic research, designing a training curriculum, or developing a weapons system, the work is implemented by means of teams. Clearly an important determinant of project success, then, is the effective functioning of teams. Effective project management thus requires that organizations identify, nurture, and assess team competence.

This and the following chapter examine team competence by raising three basic questions: What is team competence? What must teams do to perform competently? and How does one assess whether a team is performing competently?

The first question is fairly easy to address. Competent teams are able to provide solutions *faster, cheaper,* and *better* than run-of-the-mill teams. Thus team competence can be defined as those traits that enable teams to operate quickly and cost-effectively and to develop superior solutions to problems. The second question is a bit more difficult to answer because there is no single universally valid response. As these chapters show, some teams achieve competence by strengthening controls while others achieve it by loosening them and following Tom Peters's (1994) dictum to become *dis*organized. The third question is also difficult to answer. Assessing human performance is always tricky, for a number of reasons. Are the assessment instruments valid? Are the assessors capable of performing their job properly? Are the people being evaluated cooperating with the evaluation? If the answer to any of these questions is no, the value of the assessment is dubious.

Before addressing these three basic questions on team competence, it is helpful to understand what teams are and why they are so important in today's business climate. The current chapter examines the whys and wherefores of teams; the next chapter explores in detail what team competence entails.

What Is a Team?

The idea of *team* is one that most of us are comfortable with, because we come into contact with teams continually in our lives. When we turn on the television, we are likely to encounter sports teams at work—in basketball, soccer, football, rugby, cricket, and so on. If we served in the military, during basic training we were drilled on the importance of teamwork. At the office we may be members of a project team whose goal is to produce solutions that will lead to customer delight. After work we may be volunteer members of the high school parent-teacher association task force organizing a school fundraising affair.

Today, business activity is increasingly being carried out through the use of teams. There are many reasons for this. For example, a team is quite flexible; its members are assigned to it in accordance with their skills, and if the skills requirements change, it is a fairly simple matter to change the composition of the team to reflect the new requirements. Teams also enable organizations to deal with issues that lie outside the problem-solving abilities of individuals or traditional business groups. They enable organizations to add both breadth and depth to decision making.

At the highest conceptual level, teams can be defined as collections of men and women who work together to achieve a common goal. Interestingly, this definition displays a strong affinity for the Latin root of the word *competence—competere,* noted in Chapter One, which means "to strive together." Clearly teamwork entails team members striving together to achieve their goals. Although this broad definition gives a sense of what teams are, in their book *The Wisdom of Teams,* Katzenbach and Smith (1993) suggest that such a definition masks some distinctions that it might be good to highlight about how teams actually function. They have identified five levels of group activity that are affiliated with team effort.

They call the first level the *working group.* At this level, members interact primarily to share information. They do not possess a strong commitment to work together to achieve defined performance objectives. In fact, they do not even agree on what the performance objectives should be.

The second level is called the *pseudo team*. In this case, the group *could* achieve defined performance goals by working together harmoniously, but it does not. It may call itself a team but its members have little interest in shaping a common purpose. Basically, the group members pursue their individual goals. Katzenbach and Smith are highly critical of pseudo teams and opine that such groups have negative synergy such that the total group effort is less than the sum of individual efforts.

The third level of group activity is called the *potential team*. In this instance, team members recognize the importance of working together to achieve their performance goals in a coordinated and effective way, but they have not yet developed a common approach to achieving collective accountability.

The fourth level is the *real team*. Here team members are fully committed to following defined procedures and working together to achieve agreed-upon performance objectives. Furthermore, they find themselves mutually accountable to achieving them. They are a significant unit of effective performance.

The fifth level of group activity is the *high-performance team*. This is a real team in which team members possess supercommitment to doing the team's work and in which this commitment becomes transcendent. High-performance teams possess an abundance of synergy, by which the collective effort generates results that outstrip any reasonable expectation of what the team can accomplish.

The central point here is that there is more to a team than a collection of people. Five people together in an elevator do not constitute a team. If, however, the elevator should break down and the five people operate collectively to deal with the breakdown, then they have become a team. What makes the difference between a mere collection of people and a true team is tied to defining a goal that the people agree is worth pursuing through cooperative effort.

Team Efficiency

In 1987 I developed the concept of *team efficiency* in an attempt to assess the extent to which a collection of people working together are functioning effectively as a team (Frame, 1995). This concept is based on the premise that ultimately *the value of a team is defined by its performance.* This reality is often lost sight of today, a time when many team-building efforts focus on making team members feel good about themselves and their colleagues. I have recently served on teams where far more time was spent getting people to "bond" than getting down to business. Teams should not be created to serve as social clubs! They exist to produce results. Consequently, in reviewing team effectiveness, attention should zero in on results.

In engineering, efficiency is measured as the ratio of output to input. Efficiency is low when people work hard (input) and produce meager results (output). It is high when the results achieved (output) correspond closely to the effort made to produce the results (input). For example, if a device uses one hundred energy units of coal (input) to produce ninety energy units of electricity (output), it is operating at a high efficiency level of 90 percent. Conversely, if the one hundred energy units of input produce only twenty energy units of electricity, then efficiency is a meager 20 percent.

It is impossible to measure project team input and output precisely, so treatment of team efficiency is necessarily rough. For purposes of discussion, team efficiency can be loosely defined as the proportion of *potential* team performance that is *actually* achieved. (Interestingly, this mirrors the approach taken by Jaques and Cason [1994] to defining human capability. These authors direct their attention to understanding the gap between individuals' *applied capability* and their *potential capability*.) Thus if a team is accomplishing only a small portion of what it could accomplish, team efficiency is said to be low. This corresponds roughly to what Katzenbach and Smith's *working group* would be expected to achieve. Conversely, if a team is achieving as much as is physically possible, it can be said that team efficiency is high. This corresponds roughly to Katzenbach and Smith's *high-performance team.*

In mechanical systems there are two leading sources of inefficiency: machine design and friction. Poorly designed machines do not operate optimally. However, even a well-designed machine will perform suboptimally if it is not lubricated properly; performance will be constrained by excessive friction. Similarly, we see how poor organizational design and organizational friction can contribute to the suboptimal performance of project teams. For example, a team structure that keeps key project workers isolated from customers may lead to low team performance; or excessive paperwork requirements may heighten organizational friction, thus slowing the team's ability to respond effectively to job requirements.

Real-World Teams

If all the world's teams looked and operated like a professional basketball team, the issue of identifying team competence would be quite simple. Consequently, it would also be a relatively simple matter to prescribe actions that would enhance competent behavior.

Consider some of the characteristics of a professional basketball team:

- Team membership is quite stable.
- All of the team's players are world-class—the best in the business.
- The team members *want* to be part of the team—they are highly motivated.
- The rewards for team membership are generous—most professional basketball players are multimillionaires.
- Backup players exist, and they are of nearly the same caliber as the first-string team members.
- Teamwork is achieved through constant drilling.
- The goals of the game are crystal clear—to win.
- It is easy to measure the extent to which the team is achieving its primary goal—a review of the game's score is all it takes.
- The rules of the game are constant, no matter where the game is being played.
- Coaches are bosses in the traditional sense—they have the power to reward and punish the players.

What we have here is a well-defined, stable environment in which teamwork can be carried out in a straightforward fashion. An additional nice feature of this environment is that it is simple to measure the performance of individual players as well as the performance of the overall team. The statistics that are maintained game by game highlight such things as the number of baskets scored by individuals, the percentage of shots that lead to a score, the number of shots blocked, the number of assists that lead to a score, and so forth. Katzenbach and Smith (1993) tell us that team effectiveness is totally tied to performance, and with basketball teams performance is easily measured.

Unfortunately, few business environments possess the degree of stability and clarity found in professional basketball. One of the chief characteristics of today's business climate is messiness. Little is certain. In addition, team structures tend to be dynamic, with team membership constantly changing. This situation is further confused by the fact that in most cases it is difficult to measure the performance of both individuals and the whole team. For example, how can profitability levels be linked to the activities of a specific team? Or how are the contributions of the engineers, salespeople, and operations people to project success distinguished?

Despite all the hyperbole about the miracles of teamwork, the reality of teams in action suggests that it is not easy to put together effective team-based solutions to problems. Anyone who has worked extensively on teams knows that effective teamwork does not occur automatically. In an interview with *PM Network* magazine (Cabanis, 1997), Scott Adams, creator of the successful *Dilbert* comic strip and a former project manager at Pacific Bell, expressed a cynical view of how teams are implemented in organizations. When asked whether he thought teams really get things done, he responded, "Oh, sure. There's the infighting, the bickering, the sabotaging coworkers to get more resources for yourself. . . . Teams are a whirlwind of activity." Some of the difficulties in implementing team-based solutions to problems are also captured in Steven Rayner's book *Team Traps: Survival Stories from Team Disasters, Near-Misses, Mishaps, and Other Near-Death Experiences* (1996).

I suspect that in today's messy world, Katzenbach and Smith's ideal *real teams* and *high-performing teams* are especially difficult to realize, because not many teams operate with the level of stability and clarity needed to allow them to exist in the form posed by Katzenbach and Smith. Any attempt to identify the characteristics of team competence and to offer guidance on achieving competency must take into account today's confused business realities.

What Do Teams Look Like?

Teams can assume a wide variety of appearances. For example, they vary in size, ranging from two-person entities to those with much larger numbers of members. They vary in decision-making processes, ranging from highly democratic self-managed teams to autocratic undertakings. They also vary in how communications channels are configured, ranging from wheel-like configurations, where information flows down spokes through a central hub, to highly decentralized configurations.

The architecture of a team, reflected in its physical appearance, can have a dramatic impact on how it performs. In *Reframing Organizations,* Bolman and Deal (1997) illustrate this point by contrasting the architecture of a baseball team with that of a basketball team. Baseball is a slow-paced game that depends heavily on individual effort. Winning teams are those that have a strong pitching staff, some power hitters, many consistent hitters who can get on base, and players who do not commit errors. The ties that hold team players together can be quite loose.

In contrast, basketball is a fast-paced game that depends heavily on the players functioning as a single unit. Split-second decisions are the rule, so the players operate largely on the basis of a collective instinct that has been nurtured by constant drilling. Although it is certainly helpful to have a superstar to give the team an edge over its competitors, the pursuit of individual effort will not forge a winning team. In basketball, the ties that hold team players together must be quite tight. In this case, the motto of Alexander Dumas's three musketeers holds: all for one and one for all.

Models of Project Teams

Up until now, the discussion of teams has been rather abstract. This section examines some specific team structures employed to carry out project work. The list is not exhaustive. Rather, it simply illustrates various approaches taken to conduct project work and suggests the strengths and weaknesses of each approach.

Matrix Structure

A dominant reality of project teams is that most of them are created in a *matrix environment.* In matrix management, cross-functional teams comprising borrowed resources are put together. For example, testing personnel are borrowed temporarily from the testing shop. They are brought on board the project to do their testing work, and when they have completed this work they are sent home to the testing shop. Design personnel are borrowed from the design shop. Implementers come from various implementation shops within the organization—and so on.

Matrix management encompasses three sets of players. First, there are the *borrowed resources,* the men and women who carry out the project effort (such as testers, designers, and implementers). Second, there are the *project managers,* the men and women put in charge of getting the job done on time, within budget, and according to specifications. Third, there are the *functional managers,* the men and women who are the immediate supervisors of the borrowed resources. The matrix structure presents opportunities for and challenges to each of these players.

Matrix management is being promoted on a large-scale today for a number of reasons. First, it is seen as an effective way to use resources efficiently. When you need a resource, you get a hold of it and use it. When you are done with it, you send it home. This approach contrasts sharply with the more traditional team structure in which team members are semipermanent participants who stick with the project throughout its life. A problem with the traditional approach is that it employs team members both before and after they have made their key contributions to the team effort. Although such an approach helps nurture team spirit, it may not be a cost-effective use of scarce resources.

A second strength of matrix management is that it promotes cross-functional solutions to problems, which is important in today's world, where the problems we face can be quite complex and resist simpleminded solutions. In traditional approaches, a technical problem might be put into the hands of the engineering department. Although the engineering team might have important insights on the technical aspects of solving the problem, they are unlikely to appreciate the customer relations, financial, and maintenance aspects of the solution. Matrix management enables organizations to use temporarily whatever resources are deemed appropriate.

Third, matrix management may enable employees to grow on the job through job assignments that expose them to different parts of the organization and to different skill sets.

Although the advantages of the matrix approach are evident, it should be noted that the matrix structure creates serious difficulties for team building. Consider some of the problems built into the matrix structure:

Problems among the borrowed resources. The project staff who serve as borrowed resources have many complaints about the matrix approach. Their primary concern is, How will I be evaluated for my work? The project managers overseeing teams' work are seldom qualified to evaluate the efforts of individual team members because they lack the technical knowledge to assess the workers' capabilities. By the same token, workers' functional managers are in no position to evaluate team members' work because they have not directly observed the work that has been done.

The matrix structure presents team members with many other problems, including that the new project assignment may distract them from doing their core work, they seldom see projects carried out from beginning to end, they have multiple bosses, and they spend inordinate amounts of time getting up to speed on new assignments.

Problems encountered by project managers. The two most significant problems that project managers encounter with the matrix structure are getting *who* they need *when* they need them, and motivating the borrowed resources to do a good job. Both of these problems reflect the fact that project managers have little or no direct control over the resources with which they must work.

Functional manager problems. Functional managers face a number of problems in the matrix environment. One is loss of control over the activities and professional development of their workers. Other difficulties include logistical problems in responding to requests for resources and trouble evaluating the work efforts of their employees.

Disorganized Structure

In *The Tom Peters Seminar* (1994), Peters urges organizations to promote disorganization and to engage in perpetual revolution. His ideal environment is one in which work is carried out through projects and in which project leaders operate as entrepreneurs and mini-CEOs. In this environment, power resides with the project teams and is shared only sparingly with the organization's center.

An example of the Tom Peters ideal is found in Oticon, a Danish company that designs and manufactures hearing aids (Labarre, 1996). The company underwent a major revolution in 1990 when its new leader, Lars Kolind, abolished the company's formal organizational structure. In Kolind's new approach, the functional-departmental orientation disappeared. Work at headquarters became project focused, with one hundred projects being carried out concurrently.

Oticon's projects make heavy use of roving, borrowed resources, so the company has adopted a free-form matrix structure. Team members move from project to project flexibly. They are aided in this movement by the use of computer and telecommunications technology. For example, all employees at headquarters are equipped with cellular phones, so they are not tied down to one physical office location. In addition, Oticon operates a paperless environment in which all incoming paper documents are scanned and stored in a central computer. Consequently, employees can access remotely whatever information they need by using a computer from anywhere within or outside headquarters. As with the cellular phones, this access frees them from the constraints of a physical office location. The only office furniture employees need are small, wheeled caddies that have space for about thirty file folders and can be conveniently moved around the building.

At Oticon, project leaders possess compelling ideas. To gain support for these ideas, they must sell them to a ten-person management committee that controls corporate resources. In addition, in order to attract workers to become team members, project leaders must convince their colleagues that their ideas are good.

It is interesting to speculate whether this will become a dominant team structure for knowledge-based organizations in the future. Clearly the structure cannot be applied universally to all projects. It is difficult to visualize a project team building a cathedral with such a structure! However, it may lend itself to the implementation of smaller knowledge-based projects in the areas of design, research and development, marketing, and curriculum development.

Projectized Teams

Projects that last longer than several weeks may be structured as projectized efforts. Projectized teams are those to which the team members are assigned to work full-time for the duration of the project. On such teams the project manager behaves as a mini-CEO and has some control over budgets, material resources, and the performance appraisal reviews of team members. Ideally team members are collocated so they have a sense of belonging to a discrete group and lose the feeling that they are merely borrowed resources.

A well-known example of a projectized team, introduced in Chapter One, was the team IBM put together in the late 1970s to develop the IBM PC. For the duration of the project, the project manager "owned" the project resources. Team members were collocated in a warehouse in Boca Raton, Florida. Freed from the normal bureaucratic strictures of IBM, they produced the IBM PC desktop computer—a device that has revolutionized how we conduct our business and live our lives.

The chief strengths of the projectized structure are that it provides a stable environment for conducting project work and enables project managers to exercise some measure of authority in dealing with team members and colleagues throughout the organization. The projectized structure is no panacea, however. Acquiring high-quality personnel for the duration of the project may be difficult, because functional managers will be reluctant to release their best workers for prolonged periods. Once personnel are assigned to the project, the project manager must be sensitive to the anxieties that personnel may have about being cut off from their functional homes. Many team members will raise the question, Does anyone remember me back in my functional department?

Co-Responsibility Teams

In the information technology (IT) community, the 1990s saw the rapid emergence of teams headed by pairs of managers—one with technical skills, the other with business skills. This approach arose naturally as it became increasingly obvious that the traditional approach of putting a technical person in charge of running a project was not working very well in an era in which customer satisfaction was the primary objective of project efforts. Regrettably, technical managers often lack the people and business skills needed to deliver customer-focused solutions. By the same token, it does not make sense for project teams to be headed by business managers who possess limited understanding of the technical nature of the work. With co-responsibility teams, the theory is that a manager with good people and business skills can compensate for whatever deficiencies a technical manager might have in these areas, while a manager with solid technical insights can compensate for whatever technical deficiencies his or her business partner might possess.

The consequences of implementing this approach are predictable. The first question that arises when co-responsibility teams are formed is, Who is in charge? Technical managers often express disdain for the technical shortcomings of their business-focused partner. They may feel that, in the final analysis, business issues are subsidiary to technical issues. The business-focused partner, in turn, may scoff at the technologist's lack of business and people skills.

The correct answer to the question, Who is in charge? is that *both* the technical and business managers are in charge. There are plenty of success stories of projects employing co-responsibility teams. The key to this success is recognition that both the technical manager and the business manager have important contributions to make to the project.

Customer-Focused Teams

The co-responsibility team structure challenges the view that one individual—a project manager—possesses all the skills and insights needed to manage project work. This idea can be extended easily to the proposition that even two people are not enough. In the 1990s it became obvious that on many project teams it was impossible to find one or two individuals who could carry out the whole range of project management functions effectively. Consequently, a number of organizations experimented with sharing project management responsibilities among three or more people.

NCR Corporation addressed this insight in the early 1990s by creating customer-focused teams (CFTs). These teams comprise a stable group of members who come from different backgrounds and who can collectively manage the intricacies of today's complex projects. On a typical team, one member might come from the sales department, another from the technical group, and another from operations. The CFT also has a titular project manager who is not the team's boss but rather a facilitator who is first among equals.

Proponents of the CFT approach recognize that there is more to project management than creating PERT charts. Project success requires vigilant monitoring of customer needs and wants, and salespeople are often in the best position to determine what these are. The solutions that emerge from the project must ultimately be implemented effectively, and operations people often have the best insights as to what this entails. And of course project solutions usually have a technical component, so it is wise to take into account the insights of a technically capable person.

Experience shows that cross-functional CFTs can indeed take a three-dimensional view of the project, which is good. The principal problem with implementing CFTs is that the stable teams are not so stable after all. There is a tendency to pull team members off the CFT when crises elsewhere demand their services. When this happens, the CFT reverts to being a typical matrix operation.

Surgical Teams

In what has become a project management classic, *The Mythical Man-Month,* Frederick Brooks (1975) describes an approach, introduced in Chapter Two, that IBM employed in structuring some of its more significant software development projects back in the days when it dominated the computer market. What Brooks calls the *surgical team structure* (its actual name is the *chief programmer team structure* and it was originally posed by Harlan Mills) takes its rationale from the surgical theater in medicine, where a surgeon has total control in conducting a medical operation. In developing software, chief programmers—who can produce far better code than average programmers, and quickly—function like surgeons. They are given full control over producing the deliverable.

To enable them to do what they do best—write software code—they are buffered from mundane administrative chores. Thus routine editing, budget preparations, and other administrative activities are carried out by administrative staff attached to the project. The "surgeons" are also given solid technical support in the form of specialists who can give them whatever insights and assistance is deemed appropriate. For example, a testing specialist may help the chief programmer test the evolving code, and a software language specialist may offer insights into the intricacies of arcane coding.

The strengths of this team structure are obvious. For one thing, the surgeons are superperformers who are supported in doing what they do best. A good surgeon with solid support may be able to develop truly miraculous results, bypassing the hazards of development by committee. Another strength is that the deliverable is likely to be internally consistent because it has been produced by one individual. An old software adage holds that "bugs arise at the interfaces." In the surgical team structure there are not many human interfaces, so the surgeon can produce a reasonably bug-free solution.

The weaknesses of the surgical team structure are equally obvious. For example, in this structure all of the organization's eggs are placed in one basket. What if the surgeon leaves the organization? What if he or she has an ill-conceived solution? If there are any problems with the surgeon, the project is in serious trouble. Another common complaint about this structure focuses on its elitist nature. The surgeon gets all the glory while the other team members can be treated as supernumeraries. Having interviewed support staff on more than thirty surgical teams, I know that many of them question whether what they worked on was a *real team* in the sense developed by Katzenbach and Smith (1993). That is, they felt they had little or no role to play in defining the project's output. Basically they saw themselves as the servants of the surgeon.

The types of projects that lend themselves to the surgical team structure are those that entail high levels of intellectual effort. As indicated earlier, software projects can employ the surgical team approach. Beyond this, projects involving design work or research can use the surgical team structure because the success of these projects is often tied to the special insights and effective performance of a small number of superperformers. I know from personal experience that this approach underlies the writing of most books. From the perspective of a book author, it is generally easier for individuals to write books alone—assuming they have the proper support to do their jobs—than to work with coauthors, where coordination and compromise can make the writing task difficult.

Self-Managed Teams

The polar opposite of the surgical team is the *self-managed team,* also called the *self-directed work team.* In this structure, team members *collectively* assume decision-making authority. Although management writers in the 1990s saw this concept as a fresh new approach to managing work (see, for example, Wellins, Byham, and Wilson, 1991), it has in fact been around for quite some time.

An early exegesis describing the advantages of self-managed team efforts was made by Gerald Weinberg in his classic book, *The Psychology of Computer Programming* (1971). Weinberg was concerned with the fact that most software projects fail. That is, they are never finished, or else they produce deliverables that are not used. He attributes a leading cause of failure to the fact that people's egos get in the way of developing good systems. For example, team members may not function in a collaborative fashion, they may refuse to share their insights and skills with others, or they may suffer from "the pride of authorship." Weinberg concluded that the best way to deal with these ego problems is to create *egoless teams.* His egoless teams are closely akin to the self-managed teams of today. They require that team members suppress their egos and work to achieve the high-level goals needed to develop good project solutions.

It is interesting to note that nearly a quarter of a century after Weinberg's work was published, a study carried out by the Standish Group (1994) found that only a small minority (16 percent) of IT project teams get the job done on time, within budget, and according to specifications. As the saying goes, the more things change, the more they stay the same!

Self-managed teams can be configured in many different ways. In some cases they involve team members making all significant decisions, including hiring and firing decisions. In other cases, decision-making authority is limited to dealing with narrowly defined technical issues.

In theory, the idea of self-management appears to be enlightened, because it corresponds with the view that if men and women are given control over their destinies, they will rise to the occasion and become superperformers. Regrettably, the reality of self-management is less sanguine. For example, it is not clear that the majority of workers are willing to assume the responsibility of making major decisions. I once encountered a man who had been a worker at a printing company who told me that when a new management team introduced self-management at his company, the employees saw it as a trap designed to get them into trouble if they made poor decisions. Consequently, they refused to cooperate with the new management team. They preferred an approach in which they were told what to do.

Another difficulty with employing self-management is tied to the fact that effective self-managed teams cannot be created overnight. Team members need time to get accustomed to each other. Experience suggests that it takes at least a year to forge an effective self-managed team. In today's world of constant change, however, it is rare for a team to stay together for more than a few weeks or months.

Traditional Construction Teams

Architectural structures have been built by means of teams for a long time. Today the team usually comprises four sets of players: the owner (the individual or group that is paying the bills and that will eventually take over control of the deliverable), the architect-engineer (the individual or group that designs the structure and has responsibility for maintaining its integrity as the project is carried out), the general contractor (the individual or group that has ultimate responsibility for building the structure), and subcontractors (the individuals or groups that actually build the structure).

The construction effort can be configured in many different ways. Traditionally, the responsibility for the architectural integrity of the structure was given to the architect-engineer, while the responsibility for building the structure rested with the general contractor. Both players reported to the owner. Clearly this approach can lead to discontinuities in the efforts of the architect-engineer and the general contractor.

Other approaches give overall responsibility to the architect-engineer (so that the general contractor serves a subordinate role), the general contractor (so that the architect-engineer serves a subordinate role), or to an outside project management specialist (so that both the architect-engineer and the general contractor play subordinate roles).

Virtual Teams

In 1988, a leading manufacturer of computers approached our project management group at George Washington University to see whether by using existing networking technology we could enable geographically dispersed project team members to work together as if they were collocated. In the words of an executive of the company, "Our projects often entail the sales staff in the Northeast ordering equipment from our manufacturing facility in the Southwest. The equipment is then configured for customer use through the efforts of our systems engineers in the Northeast and our design team in California. What we need is to bring these people together electronically, enabling them to operate as if there were no geographical constraints."

After looking into this matter briefly, we determined that the technology was not sufficiently developed to create what today we call a *geographically dispersed virtual team*. A few years after we examined this possibility, however, developments on the Internet coupled with advances in network applications such as Lotus Notes made the creation of virtual teams realistic. Today projects can readily be carried out "virtually."

On virtual teams, team members share project data even when they are geographically dispersed. Meetings can be held via videoconferencing or teleconferencing. They can even be held using e-mail, where there is no face-to-face interaction.

Clearly, operating in a virtual team environment presents interesting team-building challenges.

Conclusions

Today's complex world and the need for speedy decisions increasingly require that people work in teams. Anyone who has worked on a high-performing team has experienced the excitement of having disparate people working together to achieve results that none could achieve alone.

But let's not be naive. Effective teamwork is difficult to achieve. Following are some pitfalls that should be addressed consciously:

The groupthink trap. We have all experienced the perils of groupthink. A colleague of mine, Jerry Harvey, has even written a bestselling (and humorous) book on one aspect of groupthink, *The Abilene Paradox and Other Meditations* (1996). With groupthink, innovation is squelched. While visiting a major university, I once witnessed the efforts of a committee that worked two years to reform its doctoral program. Periodically, committee progress would be reported to the faculty. Regrettably, in an effort to achieve consensus among the disparate committee members, any initiatives that displayed a smidgeon of innovation were jettisoned. At the end of the two-year process, the committee generated a report that an eighteen-year-old could have drafted during a weekend while watching MTV and chatting with friends on the phone.

Decision paralysis. To the extent that teamwork demands that team members do not have a strong degree of consensus in making judgments, decision making may stretch out interminably, particularly when consensus is not achieved immediately. The team members allow different parties to articulate their views, then they discuss them in an open debate. An informal poll may be taken to see whether consensus is being achieved. If it is not, the contending parties are given another chance to speak their mind, a new informal poll is taken, and so on.

Balancing the need for individual recognition with the need for group work. Since before the time of the ancient Greeks and Hebrews, Western culture has emphasized the place of the individual in society. From the time they are children, Westerners are taught to believe that their opinions count and they are encouraged to strive to achieve individual recognition. Teamwork, however, emphasizes the achievements of the group over those of the individual. This group focus can create problems for men and women nurtured on the importance of individualism.

Rewarding team versus individual performance. Given the emphasis on individual achievement in the West, rewards for high performance are typically offered to individuals. Employee-of-the-month awards, individual performance bonuses, and job promotions for good work are obvious examples of this phenomenon. However, in a perceptive article appearing in *Harvard Business Review,* Alfie Kohn (1993) shows how these types of rewards for individuals can lead to distortions in behavior as employees become more focused on achieving rewards than on doing a good job for the job's sake. He also shows how these rewards can lead to resentment among the employees who are not rewarded. If we are going to get serious about working on teams, we must learn how to use group rewards more effectively.

Chapter Ten

Assessing Team Competence

The primary objective of this chapter is to identify an approach to assessing team competence. Of the three levels of competence explored in this book—the level of individuals, of teams, and of the organization—team competence is the trickiest to address. As shown in earlier chapters, a number of tried-and-true approaches can be taken to assess the competence of individuals, such as exams, interviews, and observation of behavior over time; and the next chapter shows that in recent years useful models have been developed to assess organizational competence, such as the Capability Maturity Model and the assessment processes associated with ISO 9000, the Deming Prize, and the Baldrige Award. But regrettably, widely accepted generic techniques to assess project team performance have not been developed. This shortfall is a consequence of at least two facts: that it is difficult to measure the results of project team efforts accurately, and that it is difficult to visualize what an ideal work team should look like. Each of these issues is discussed in this chapter.

Difficulties in Measuring and Assessing Project Team Results

Team competence is tied to the *results* of team efforts. Competent teams consistently produce good results, whereas incompetent teams do not. Beyond this, competent teams operate at high levels of efficiency. That is, their actual output is close to the maximum output they are capable of producing.

This view of team competence has two practical problems associated with it. First, it is difficult to determine whether the team's outputs meaningfully reflect good or bad work effort. Consider the following example that represents a situation commonly encountered today. In negotiating a contract with a client, the sales representative promises that the project team will do a ten-month job in six months. If the team does the job in eight months, they have failed to achieve the six-month target established for them. As a consequence of the two-month "delay," the client expresses dissatisfaction with the team's effort.

Did the team do a bad job? After all, they performed their work two months faster than the ten-month standard. One could convincingly argue that the team performed superlatively and that the real failure here was the unrealistic promises made by the sales representative. How should this kind of ambiguity be dealt with in assessing team competence?

Second, it is difficult to assess the extent to which project success or failure is tied to the team's effort, or to the efforts of an account executive, or to the adequacy of the organization's information systems, or to the availability of up-to-date technology, and so on. It is easy to imagine a situation in which a mediocre team scores a big success because the processes and technology with which they work make failure nearly impossible. By the same token, life is filled with stories of capable people who fail to achieve their goals because they were not provided with the tools needed to do a good job. How should we deal with this kind of ambiguity in assessing team competence?

Difficulties in Visualizing the Ideal Team

As the last chapter illustrated, teams can be configured in many different ways. In matrix teams, team members are borrowed resources who are brought onto the project, do their jobs, and then return to their functional homes. In co-responsibility teams, team efforts are headed by two people—a development manager and a business manager. In customer-focused teams, the project effort is guided by what amounts to a cross-functional steering committee composed of representatives from different functional departments.

The number of ways in which project teams can be configured is limited only by the imagination. The point is that there is no ideal team structure that provides a benchmark against which organizations can assess the performance of specific teams. When considering team structure, *situational management* is the rule.

Because there is no ideal team structure that can serve as a benchmark, attention should be focused on identifying the *functions* carried out by the project team, regardless of the specific nature of the team structure. For example, does the team have clearly defined goals that its members can pursue? Does it have a clearly defined communication plan? Are team members supplied with the proper tools to do their jobs?

Criteria for Assessing Team Competence

Research and experience show that a number of criteria can be applied to assessing team performance that identify the level of team competence regardless of how the team is structured. Good teams have the following characteristics:

- Clear and realistic goals
- Well-defined deliverables
- A proper mix of skills
- A proper level of education and skills among team members
- Adequate tools to do the job
- Discipline (such as a communication plan, regular meetings, and well-defined documentation requirements)
- Cohesion and the capacity to reach consensus readily
- Effective leadership
- Chutzpah
- A structure appropriate to the work that needs to be done
- The ability to integrate diversity
- The ability to achieve the desired results
- The ability to work with customers effectively

Each of these characteristics is discussed in turn.

Clear and Realistic Goals

In the 1950s, Peter Drucker, the progenitor of much modern management practice, became a missionary who proselytized the gospel of *management by objectives,* or MBO (1954). Drucker recognized that *objectives* (or goals or targets) establish the cadence that enables people in organizations to march to the same drumbeat. When individuals march to a personal drumbeat, chaos results. When they march to a clearly defined, universally held drumbeat, they can create a formidable marching band.

This reality holds true for project teams. How clear are the project's goals? Are they implied or are they described explicitly? How well communicated are they? Are team members aware of them? Clearly, if project goals are ill defined, it is difficult for teams to operate competently.

The need for clear goals is also emphasized by Katzenbach and Smith in their book *The Wisdom of Teams* (1993). These authors point out that in the final analysis, successful teams are those that have a strong sense of where they are headed and thus can achieve their performance objectives. For performance objectives to be achievable, they must be well defined.

Creating clearly defined goals is often easier said than done. What may be crystal clear to the progenitor of a goal may be viewed as a turgid morass by its intended audience. Over the years a consensus has emerged on the central characteristic of a clear goal (or objective, target, or requirement): *a goal is clear when, after being reviewed by a group of people, the group holds a single opinion on its meaning.* (Consider the opposite situation: five people, when shown a goal, interpret it in five different ways; this goal obviously lacks clarity.)

How can a clear goal be created? The answer: make the goal verifiable. The standard way to do this is to make the goal measurable. To illustrate this point, contrast the following two formulations of a goal set by a college swimming coach:

Formulation A: to swim the pool as fast as possible

Formulation B: to swim four laps of the twenty-five-meter pool using the freestyle stroke in one minute or less by May 5

Formulation A can be interpreted in many ways. One swimmer may define "as fast as possible" to mean "give it your best shot," whereas another may define it as "exceed the current record for our swimming league." One swimmer may assume that the coach is talking about a two-lap sprint, whereas another may prepare for an eight-lap event.

In contrast, Formulation B is quite clear. There is still some room for interpretation (such as, "Am I permitted to wear flippers?" or "Will the pool be filled with water?"), but the likelihood of misunderstanding the intent of the goal is quite low.

It is not sufficient simply to have clearly defined goals. They must be realistic as well. The goal "To end all human suffering" is a noble one, but it is simply not achievable. When unrealistic goals are established, team failure is hardwired to the project before any work has begun.

The MBO approach offers a way to increase the realism of goals: in creating the goals, the people who need the job to be done need to work together with the people who will do the work. The former have a sense of what should be done, but generally they lack a realistic sense of how to achieve it. The latter may know precisely what it takes to do a job but lack the big-picture perspective to frame the goals in an effective way. Once agreement on what the goals should be has been achieved, both parties should sign a contract. In this contract, the project workers promise to do everything possible to achieve the goals while their clients (possibly senior levels of management) promise to supply whatever support is needed to enable the workers to do their jobs.

Well-Defined Deliverables

The outputs of the team effort (its deliverables) must be well defined. The characteristics of the deliverable are captured in its requirements. These are frequently broken into two categories: *functional* requirements and *technical* requirements.

Functional requirements describe in ordinary language what the deliverable will look like and what it will do. For example, the functional requirements associated with building a new shopping mall would include the following type of statement: "The mall will comprise thirty stores selling a wide variety of products, ranging from specialty food products to clothing to consumer electronics to books and stationery. At least ten of these stores should be nationally recognized vendors." The functional requirement can incorporate artists' conceptual drawings of what the mall will look like.

Technical requirements describe what the deliverable will look like and what it will do in precise technical terms. In the shopping mall example, one technical requirement might be, "Flooring for the mall common areas will be made of Tuff Tile eighteen-inch square tiles in the Mocha Delight color." The physical dimensions and other technical features of each store can be captured in blueprints and electrical wiring diagrams.

There is more to defining deliverables than detailing their functional and technical requirements. The deliverables must also be defined in terms of scheduled delivery dates and cost constraints. Are project team members aware of the scheduled delivery dates and committed to meeting them? Similarly, are they sensitive to cost constraints?

The extent to which deliverables can be well defined varies from discipline to discipline. Routine projects, such as the installation of automatic teller machines in banks, lend themselves to clear definition of what the deliverables should look like and what they should do, in both a functional and a technical sense. In contrast, research and development projects, such as a project to define the causes of a disease, are carried out in an amorphous fashion, analogous to an explorer venturing into unknown territory without a map. Here the deliverables may be hard to define precisely. Although general functional requirements may be relatively easy to lay out ("investigate arthropod-borne viruses"), the technical details may be tricky to nail down due to lack of specific information on how things will work out.

Proper Mix of Skills

A truism in today's complex world is that solutions to problems require cross-functional inputs. Obviously, in a project to build a bridge, engineering experts are needed in a wide array of areas, including specialists in laying the foundation, structural engineers, road-building specialists, and so on. But also needed are additional specialists from outside the technical area. For example, contract specialists, purchasing specialists, account executives, accountants, maintenance personnel, and financial experts may be important members of such a project team.

Competent teams are composed of people with the right skills to do the job. In today's environment, in which reengineering dominates and workers are asked to "do more with less," there is a real danger that project teams will lack the proper mix of skills to carry out the job effectively. Key players may be absent from the roster while team members are encouraged to wear many hats. If the team lacks the right mix of players, it is important that they be able to access the needed people. This can be done by "borrowing" the needed skill sets from within the organization (insourcing) or by "renting" them from outside (outsourcing). Any assessment of team competence should examine carefully the skills-mix of the project team in an attempt to determine whether the right skills are being applied to the job.

An understanding of what skills need to be applied to a job requires that a conscious assessment of skill requirements be carried out. Once these skill requirements have been identified, they must be explicitly tied to the work that will be done. This matching of skills to work can be carried out by creating a *responsibility chart,* which links skills needed to the elements of the work breakdown structure.

Proper Level of Education and Skills

It is not enough to have a team composed of members possessing nominal knowledge and skills in appropriate areas. The question now is, Are the team members adequately educated and skilled to carry out their jobs effectively? Common sense suggests that in any group of people there are wide variations in capability to do work. For example, in the development of software, superprogrammers can write ten times more high-level code in a specific period than average programmers. Clearly teams with the best-educated and most highly experienced members are more likely to be high-performing teams than those with undereducated and inexperienced members.

In today's era of rapid technological change, it is unreasonable to expect that at any given moment all team members will be up to speed in the areas they are expected to master. Effective teams are those in which team members are able to upgrade their skills quickly. One way this can be done is through training. Do team members have access to the training they need, either through in-house programs or through outside training? As indicated earlier, another way for teams to upgrade skills quickly is to acquire the needed talent by insourcing or outsourcing. Is such talent accessible?

Ultimately it may be necessary to assess the level of competence of the *core team*, those people most closely associated with the project over its life. This can be done through testing, by observation of on-the-job performance, through standard performance appraisal reviews, and so on.

Adequate Tools to Do the Job

Good brains, keen insights, and high energy levels do not guarantee that the job will get done. Project team members also need to have the right tools in order to achieve their performance objectives. Just as a carpenter without a saw will be unable to cut wood properly, software developers without the right code-writing tools and team budget analysts who lack activity-based cost data will not be able to carry out their duties effectively.

A broad range of tools should be considered. For example, some tools fall in the domain of management tools. In project management, automated scheduling software, networked information systems, automated order-processing systems, and up-to-date computer and telecommunications technology are examples of management tools needed for team members to operate competently. Other tools are specific to the job being executed. If the project team needs to dig a trench, access to a well-functioning backhoe is helpful. Teams investigating the structure of viruses need access to a scanning electron microscope. High-speed computers must be available to teams attempting to simulate regional weather patterns.

If the team does not possess the right tools to do the job, can they acquire them readily? If not, it is hard to see how they can function competently in carrying out their chores.

This criterion illustrates the fact that successful project teams are dependent on a number of factors that lie outside their direct realm of control. Even smart team members cannot operate properly without the proper support. To assess team competence, it is necessary to look at external support factors because they can contribute to project success or failure.

Discipline

The triple constraints of project management are unrelenting: *schedules* must be met, work must be done within tight *budgets,* and clearly defined *specifications* must be achieved. These constraints will not be attained through good intentions. They require a strong measure of team discipline. For example, the team must establish a communication plan and stick with it, regular meetings must be held and be well attended, and documentation requirements need to be established and enforced.

The popular conception of teamwork focuses on the need for good human relations among team members. Clearly this is important. Teams filled with strife or indifference are not likely to be successful, but organizations must not let this emphasis on the human relations aspects of teams blind them to the equally important need for discipline. Both good human relations and discipline are prerequisites for project success.

Team discipline has a number of facets. For example, discipline demands the existence of appropriate methods and procedures that are strictly enforced. Without adherence to well-established methods and procedures, the team's efforts will quickly degenerate to a hodgepodge operation. Another facet concerns attention to documentation. Are the documentation requirements appropriate to the project? Do team members take documentation efforts seriously, or do they shrug them off as so much "administrivia"?

Cohesion and Capacity to Reach Consensus Readily

One of the better-known teams in literature is Alexander Dumas's three musketeers. Their motto—all for one and one for all—captures the essence of the concept of team cohesion. Cohesion stands on two legs. One is trust. On cohesive teams, the team members trust one another to meet their commitments. Without trust, divisiveness reigns and cohesiveness cannot be attained. The second leg is practice. On cohesive teams, the more experience that team members have working together, the better they will get at working together because they will become familiar with their roles and capabilities and the roles and capabilities of their comrades.

A spin-off of team cohesion is the improved ability of team members to reach consensus readily on issues requiring decisions. If I am working with a group of strangers, I have no basis for trusting their judgments. I have not worked with them previously and do not know their capabilities. If I am working with colleagues I know well from other work experiences, and if I trust their judgments and commitments and understand their capabilities, it is generally easier for the group to achieve consensus on important issues. When teams live by the motto of the three musketeers, they demonstrate a willingness to suppress their individual egos in order to meet the needs of the whole.

Effective Leadership

Team leaders can make the difference between spectacular and lackluster team performance. According to John Gardner (1989), leadership entails enabling people to achieve their potential. Gardner's attributes of leaders include such things as physical stamina, high energy levels, courage, eagerness to accept responsibility, self-confidence, competence, possession of people skills, and decisiveness.

Leadership failure can take many forms, including the following:

- The technically focused team leader who dreads dealing with nontechnical issues
- The socially inept team leader whose weak people skills cause unhappiness and low morale
- The cowardly team leader who is easily intimidated and will not stand up for what is right
- The unprepared, inexperienced team leader who has not been prepared to assume a leadership function
- The unimaginative team leader who fears any initiatives that are not "by the book"
- The autocratic team leader who neither solicits nor welcomes feedback and input from team members

The leadership challenge is especially poignant for project team leaders, because typically the team's members are borrowed resources. Consequently, team leaders do not have carrots and sticks with which to motivate team members. They are not commanders in a traditional sense, issuing orders that their minions respond to with a crisp salute and a hearty "Aye, aye." Team leaders' leadership skills rest heavily on their ability to *influence* team members over whom they have little or no direct control.

Incidentally, the ability to achieve the team cohesion mentioned earlier is closely tied to the leadership capabilities of the team leader. Like good coaches in the sports arena, good leaders are able to get a collection of people to work together effectively. When there is conflict among team members, good leaders can resolve it. When the team encounters decision gridlock, good leaders can break the gridlock and get people working together to come to a decision. When team members lose focus, good leaders can center them.

Assessing a team leader's leadership capabilities is largely a subjective affair. The assessment should certainly examine whether team members perceive the team leader as possessing good leadership capabilities.

Chutzpah

Teams with high energy levels and a bit of a swagger tend to be good candidates to become high-performing teams. In the parlance of today's street talk, they've got an attitude. The swagger is rooted in a sense of their unique identity. They are separate from the rest of the world. They are special. Some of the most formidable teams are those that have a point to prove. They operate with evangelical fervor. Common attitudes associated with such teams are illustrated by the following phrases: "Let's do it!" "To hell with the others!" and "They say it can't be done—we'll show 'em!"

Although chutzpah does not lend itself to objective measurement, it should still be one of the criteria that team assessors employ in assessing team competence. Questions that can be raised here include the following: Have the team members given themselves a team name and logo? During interviews with the assessors do they display a strong sense of team identity? Do they discuss

their teammates with admiration? Do they see the work of their
team as being special? Do they generally possess a positive attitude
toward the team and its efforts?

Appropriate Structure

The last chapter examined a number of team structures commonly employed in carrying out projects. Obviously how teams
are structured has an impact on how effectively they function.
Team structure must be appropriate to the work that needs to be
done. For example, it would be disastrous to have a single project
manager make all substantive decisions—large and small—on large
complex projects, even though this might be appropriate on
smaller, routine projects.

To assess team competence, team structure must be examined
and the match between the structure and the work needs to be determined. Key issues that should be addressed include the following: Is the degree of centralization of decision making appropriate
to the job (for example, excessive centralization or excessive employee empowerment)? Are the number of communications channels embedded in the team structure appropriate to the job (for
instance, information overload or information paucity)? Is the degree of role definition appropriate to the job (for example, excessively rigid or excessively loose role definition)?

Ability to Integrate Diversity

Teams are a collection of people each of whom brings special insights, unique experiences, and singular skills to the team effort.
They certainly are not like the interchangeable parts of a machine.
A major component of team building is to discover how to manage the diversity of team members while recognizing that diversity
is a two-edged sword. On the one hand, diversity is a strength: it
enables teams to put together different insights and skills that no
one individual possesses and can lead to creative solutions to problems. On the other hand, diversity possesses weaknesses: the multiple perspectives and different levels of capability contained in a
diverse team can lead to divisiveness and make it difficult to coor-
dinate team efforts.

The ability to manage diversity has become important today because organizations recognize that they must increasingly depend on the use of cross-functional teams. The focus on cross-functional teams reflects the complexity of today's business environment. It is not enough for project teams to be composed purely of technical people who view project work while wearing technical blinders. The team should also include members who reflect the marketing and sales perspective, the finance perspective, the interests of operations, the maintenance point of view, and so on.

Managing team diversity requires that both the team and its larger organization be open to contending points of view. This in turn means that the team must be able to reconcile different perspectives without getting bogged down in conflict. Beyond this, the team must be able to create a synthesis from the different points of view and use this synthesis as the basis of its operations.

An assessment of the team diversity criterion should address the following types of questions: What processes are in place to capture the diverse contributions of the team members? How is diversity incorporated into decision making? Overall, is the diversity a plus or a minus in the team's efforts?

Ability to Achieve Desired Results

Too often people evaluate the "goodness" of a team in terms of the ability of team members to develop good personal relations with one another. Team-building exercises typically focus on getting team members to work together, which is an admirable objective. But organizations must recognize that a team composed of men and women who have developed fast friendships and who have learned to trust and respect one another is not a success unless it achieves its performance objectives.

In the final analysis, it is results that count. Is the team consistently achieving its performance objectives? The assessment associated with this criterion should focus on tracking performance. Is the team achieving the technical requirements of the project on time and within budget and in such a way that leads to customer satisfaction? Information needed to answer this question should be readily available in weekly status reports. If the reports show that the team is not achieving its technical milestones on schedule, or if they indicate budget overruns, the project team is having difficulty achieving the desired results.

Ability to Work Effectively with Customers

It is common for project team members to view customers from an us-versus-them perspective. There are many reasons why this happens. For example, technically proficient team members may resent what they perceive to be meddling from customers who are amateurs, or they might be upset by the patronizing attitude that customers assume or by irritating customer requests that cause well-formulated plans to go awry. The problem with this perspective is that it contributes strongly to project failure.

Ultimately, project success and failure are determined by customers. It is easy to visualize a situation in which a project team meets the well-known triple constraints of project management and gets the job done on time, within budget, and according to specifications—yet still encounters failure when customers misuse or underuse the deliverable or do not use it at all. Successful project teams maintain good customer relations. They respect their customers, demonstrate patience in dealing with them, and make a special effort to communicate openly with them.

Good relations between the project team and customers does not happen automatically. Team members must be sensitized to their roles in dealing with customers. They should recognize that an important part of their jobs is to do work that leads to customer satisfaction. In addition, team members who need to interact directly with customers should establish mechanisms that ensure that open two-way communication channels have been established, enabling them to gain ready access to customers and allowing customers to reach them easily when necessary. Finally, if necessary, project team members should undertake some manner of training or should receive coaching on how to handle customer unhappiness when it arises.

Steps in Assessing Team Competence

Team-competency assessments should be carried out from time to time. It is particularly important to do this on long-term projects (say projects lasting three months or longer) and with stable teams that work together over extended periods. These team assessments serve two important functions. First, they provide those charged with the overall management of project efforts feedback on how well teams in their domain are doing their jobs. Second, they enable team members to grow aware of the fact that team competence is not an irrelevant abstraction but rather has some definable and assessable components. With this awareness, team members can develop a clear sense of what is expected of them *in their performance as a team.*

Assessment should occur at two levels. First, team members can be asked to carry out periodic self-assessments. When this should be done and what the level of detail of the self-assessment should be will of course be determined by such things as the size, length, and complexity of the project effort. For large, long-term, complex projects, the self-assessments might be bundled with other reporting requirements and might be scheduled to occur every other month. For short, well-defined projects, "quick and dirty" self-assessments may be part of the project closeout procedure.

External team competency assessments should also be carried out when appropriate. This can be done best by a cross-functional assessment group composed of people from different areas, such as engineering, information technology, sales, finance, and operations. This group would periodically interview team members and review project records in light of the team competency criteria listed earlier in this chapter in order to come to a conclusion about the team's capabilities.

Of course it would be instructive to, from time to time, compare the results of the team's self-assessment with the assessment of the external reviewers. Do the two groups share similar perspectives on the team's competence? Are there gaps between the two views, and if so, where do they appear?

Once the assessment has been carried out, it is time for action. If the assessment shows deficiencies in the team's ability to do the job, should corrective action be launched? If so, what specific steps should be taken to improve the performance of the team? When assessments are carried out for a wide range of teams and the results show serious deficiencies across the board, should this lead to the reengineering of team efforts in general?

An appendix at the end of this chapter contains a team competency assessment instrument that addresses the twelve team competency criteria discussed in this chapter. Using this instrument to evaluate team performance provides organizations with a general sense of whether they have competent teams carrying out their project efforts.

Conclusions

Although organizations have rather extensive experience assessing competence at the level of the individual (individual competence has been a topic of interest for thousands of years and was discussed in ancient times by Plato, Sun Tzu, and the Bible), and although they have gained experience in recent years in assessing competence at the organizational level through the efforts of ISO 9000, the Deming Prize, and the Capability Maturity Model, little attention has focused on examining team competence. Although some work has been done on how team-based reward systems should be implemented (a topic that touches on the periphery of team competence), little work deals directly with this topic. Given the interconnection of individual, team, and organizational competencies, it seems obvious that we must seriously develop approaches to assessing the most ignored and ephemeral level—the team.

A Team Competence Assessment Instrument

Scoring Key

1 and 2 = inadequate

3 = just adequate

4 and 5 = more than adequate

This assessment instrument examines project team competence according to a number of functions that effective project teams should be able to achieve. The instrument can be used to identify the overall degree of team competence for individual teams. It can also be employed as a diagnostic tool to identify general team strengths and weaknesses within an organization.

An assessment group should carry out interviews with team members and review pertinent team status reports before filling out the following form. Scores should be tabulated for each item. There are a total of 65 items in the form, so a total score of less than 195 (65 items × score of 3, indicating adequate performance) indicates a team that is performing in a less-than-adequate fashion overall. Beyond this aggregate view, any item with a score of 2 or less represents a trouble spot, contributing to low levels of team performance. All items with a score of 2 or less should be highlighted and corrective action should be taken to deal with them.

Assessment Criterion: Clarity of Goals

Item		Score
Clarity of overall mission of the team effort	1 2 3 4 5	__
Clarity of broad technical goals of the project	1 2 3 4 5	__
Clarity of the project time frame	1 2 3 4 5	__
Clarity of budget constraints	1 2 3 4 5	__
Clarity of who the customers are	1 2 3 4 5	__
Team members' understanding of the goals	1 2 3 4 5	__
Total		__

Assessment Criterion: Well-Defined Deliverables

Item		Score
Clear understanding by team members of what the deliverables are	1 2 3 4 5	__
Clarity of the technical requirements of the project	1 2 3 4 5	__
Clarity of the schedule requirements for key milestones	1 2 3 4 5	__
Clarity of budgets associated with work to be achieved	1 2 3 4 5	__
Total		__

Assessment Criterion: Proper Mix of Skills

Item		Score
Clarity of what skill sets are needed to do the job	1 2 3 4 5	__

Appropriateness of team skill sets for the
work to be done   1 2 3 4 5   __
Adequate number of skilled players to do
the job   1 2 3 4 5   __
Access to needed skills through outsourcing   1 2 3 4 5   __
Clear links between skills and tasks   1 2 3 4 5   __
Total   __

Assessment Criterion: Proper Level of Education and Skills

Item   Score

Clarity of the level of education and skills
needed to do the job   1 2 3 4 5   __
Adequacy of the education and skills level
of the team   1 2 3 4 5   __
Capacity to acquire needed education and
skills through training   1 2 3 4 5   __
Capacity to acquire needed education and
skills through outsourcing   1 2 3 4 5   __
Capacity to acquire needed education and
skills through insourcing   1 2 3 4 5   __
Adequate numbers of educated and skilled
players   1 2 3 4 5   __
Total   __

Assessment Criterion: Adequate Tools to Do the Job

Item   Score

Clear understanding of what tools are needed
for the job   1 2 3 4 5   __
Adequacy of tools to do the job   1 2 3 4 5   __
Capacity to acquire the right tools when
needed   1 2 3 4 5   __
Existence of activity-based accounting system   1 2 3 4 5   __
Existence of automated scheduling tools   1 2 3 4 5   __
Employment of automated scheduling tools   1 2 3 4 5   __
Total   __

Assessment Criterion: Discipline

Item		Score
Clearly defined methods and procedures	1 2 3 4 5	__
Existence of good documentation protocols	1 2 3 4 5	__
Commitment of team members to meeting documentation requirements	1 2 3 4 5	__
Adequacy of communication plan	1 2 3 4 5	__
Adequate frequency of scheduled meetings	1 2 3 4 5	__
Attendance at meetings	1 2 3 4 5	__
Total		__

Assessment Criterion: Cohesion and Capacity to Reach Consensus Readily

Item		Score
Signs of team spirit (such as team name, logo)	1 2 3 4 5	__
Speed of team-based decision making	1 2 3 4 5	__
"All for one and one for all" attitude among team members	1 2 3 4 5	__
Total		__

Assessment Criterion: Effective Leadership

Item		Score
Team leader demonstrates willingness to lead	1 2 3 4 5	__
Team leader demonstrates ability to lead	1 2 3 4 5	__
Team leader viewed as a true leader by team members	1 2 3 4 5	__
Team leader can manage conflict among team members	1 2 3 4 5	__
Team leader has respect of management	1 2 3 4 5	__
Team leader has respect of clients	1 2 3 4 5	__
Total		__

Assessment Criterion: Chutzpah

Item		Score
Sense of special character of the team	1 2 3 4 5	__

Willingness to put in whatever time it takes
to do the job   1 2 3 4 5   __
"Can-do" attitude of team members   1 2 3 4 5   __
Total   __

Assessment Criterion: Team Structure Appropriate to the Work

Item		*Score*
Existence of clearly defined team structure	1 2 3 4 5	__
Proper balance of centralization and empowerment	1 2 3 4 5	__
Right number of communications channels to conduct work most effectively	1 2 3 4 5	__
Proper balance between well-defined and loose role definition	1 2 3 4 5	__
General appropriateness of team structure to the work	1 2 3 4 5	__
Total		__

Assessment Criterion: Ability to Integrate Diversity

Item		*Score*
Decision-making process incorporates different points of view (such as technical, nontechnical, sales, finance, and so on)	1 2 3 4 5	__
Value of diversity emphasized	1 2 3 4 5	__
Diverse viewpoints incorporated to make valuable contributions to decision making	1 2 3 4 5	__
Ability of team to handle forces of divisiveness	1 2 3 4 5	__
Total		__

Assessment Criterion: Ability to Achieve Desired Results

Item		*Score*
Track record in meeting technical milestones	1 2 3 4 5	__
Track record in meeting schedule requirements	1 2 3 4 5	__
Track record in operating within budget requirements	1 2 3 4 5	__

Anticipated ability to meet future technical
milestones   1 2 3 4 5   __
Anticipated ability to meet future schedule
requirements   1 2 3 4 5   __
Anticipated ability to operate within budget
constraints   1 2 3 4 5   __
Total   __

Assessment Criterion: Customer Relations Capabilities

Item   Score

Open communication channels with
customers   1 2 3 4 5   __
Respect for customer viewpoints   1 2 3 4 5   __
Sensitivity to customer issues   1 2 3 4 5   __
Commitment to achieving customer
satisfaction   1 2 3 4 5   __
Skill in dealing with upset customers   1 2 3 4 5   __
Total   __

Grand Total Score   __

Part Four

The Project-Competent Organization

Chapter Eleven

Organizational Project Competence

Consider a hypothetical project manager, Christine, who has superlative technical skills to run projects as well as excellent people skills. She has been fortunate to work with intelligent, hardworking, highly competent team members on the projects she has managed. By anyone's reckoning, Christine and her teams should constitute "dream teams" that consistently get the job done on time, within budget, and according to specifications—and whose work leads to customer delight. The reality, however, is that Christine and her teams constantly struggle to carry out their projects and they often face schedule slippages, cost overruns, and customer discontent. What's going on here?

When this type of phenomenon occurs, it may reflect the fact that project teams and their project managers are not receiving the kinds of support they need from their organization. This is illustrated in the following three examples:

Because an organization lacks an effective project accounting system, its project teams do not have proper budget control data to check to see whether they are on target or whether they are drifting.

Because an organization lacks an effective precontract review process, sales staff continually promise customers more than project teams can deliver, thus raising customer expectations and leading to eventual customer disaffection and exasperation.

Because an organization provides its workers with antiquated tools, project teams have trouble developing high-quality results.

Clearly it is not enough simply to have the best people and the best teams working on projects. In each of the cases just cited, competent team members will experience failure because of the lack of organizational support. For organizations to produce superior solutions consistently, they themselves must display a strong measure of competence.

The idea of *organizational competence* is closely allied to Frederick Herzberg's concept of *hygiene factors*. In his well-known article on motivation, Herzberg (1968) points out that what many people consider motivators (for example, good wages, good attitudes of supervisors, and good working conditions) are not in fact true motivators. He lumps together elements such as wages, supervisor attitudes, and working conditions under the label *hygiene factors,* which are attributes that organizations should possess if they want to maintain a healthy working environment. If these factors are missing, then organizations will perform suboptimally.

This chapter explores the idea of organizational competence. It identifies what it is, how it can be assessed, and what steps can be taken to strengthen it.

Recent Focus on Organizational Competence

Japan's stunning economic successes in the 1970s and 1980s led traditional industrial players to examine why the shining performance of Japanese companies was casting a dark shadow on their operations. A comparison of Japanese and traditional Western products made it obvious why Japan was doing so well: their products were of superior quality and were offered at reasonable prices. Customers were voting with their pocketbooks. They consistently chose Japanese products over competing Western products because the former were seen to offer better value.

The ability of Japanese companies to produce high-quality products did not occur by chance. Recognizing that they had a reputation for shoddy workmanship, Japanese manufacturing enterprises systematically adopted rigorous quality assurance processes from the 1950s onward. Their efforts bore fruit in the 1970s, particularly in industries such as consumer electronics, automobiles, ceramics, and optics.

Spurred on by the Japanese example, enterprises throughout the world began reassessing their operations and commenced adopting the quality assurance approaches of their Japanese competitors. *Quality* became everyone's watchword. It served as the cornerstone of the competitive strategies of companies operating in the global marketplace. It led to the recognition of the central role of customers in business processes. It ultimately resulted in a plethora of initiatives with labels such as Total Quality Management and business process reengineering.

Most significant from the viewpoint of this book, the focus on quality stimulated inquiries into the idea of what makes organizations effective. Once again, the Japanese played a seminal role with the establishment of the Deming Prize. This prize is awarded to companies with superlative quality performance. The Deming Prize showed that it is possible to assess organizational effectiveness in a reasonably objective fashion. It does this by concentrating on ten major categories for its evaluation criteria. Organizations being reviewed are assessed on their policies, management of the organization, education, information gathering, analysis, standardization, control, quality assurance, results, and future planning (Tenner and DeToro, 1992).

The Deming Prize stimulated other efforts to create systematic procedures to assess the quality of an organization's operations, such as the ISO 9000, the Baldrige Award, and the Capability Maturity Model (CMM) initiatives.

Interest in organizational effectiveness outside the quality arena was stimulated by works written by leading management thinkers. For example, Peter Senge promotes the idea of the *learning organization* (although he did not originate this concept) in his best-selling book, *The Fifth Discipline* (1990). Senge suggests that competent organizations are those that continually learn from their experiences, enabling them to adjust effectively to the pulls and pushes of today's turbulent business environment. Senge identifies five disciplines that learning organizations must possess: systems thinking, personal mastery, building shared visions, team learning, and mental models.

The point is that by the early 1990s it had become generally accepted that to compete effectively in brutally competitive world markets, organizations must operate competently. This would enable them to produce high-quality goods and services faster, cheaper, and better than their competitors. Furthermore, their degree of competence could be assessed objectively according to some agreed-upon evaluation criteria, such as the Deming Prize's ten criteria or Senge's five disciplines.

What Is Organizational Competence?

Organizations demonstrate organizational competence when they create an environment that supports employees in doing the best job possible. Competent organizations provide their project workers with the following:

• *Clearly defined and well-formulated procedures for performing work.* Without good procedures, the organization will be like a band in which each musician is reading from a different sheet of music. It will produce a cacophony rather than a harmonious melody.

• *Access to information needed to perform work effectively.* The organization's teams need to have access to pertinent information so they can do their jobs properly. Thus information systems must be put in place so that team members can control costs, track orders, identify resource availability, and so on.

• *Sufficient quantities of qualified human and material resources.* If it takes five experienced carpenters to frame a house properly in one week, then five experienced carpenters must be supplied. Furthermore, these carpenters must be given properly maintained, up-to-date tools to do their jobs. Also, they must be provisioned with adequate supplies of lumber, nails, and other materials needed to frame houses. If sufficient quantities of qualified human and material resources are lacking, the likelihood of project failure grows astronomically.

• *Opportunities for training and education.* In today's fast-paced world where Monday's hot new innovation is Friday's historical curiosity, everyone needs to update their skills and knowledge continually. Poorly educated workers will not serve their organizations properly.

• *Clearly defined visions of where the organization is headed.* For organizations to operate effectively, their employees must have a strong sense of where the organization is headed. Otherwise, individual workers will pursue their idiosyncratic visions of what the organization's business is and chaos will ensue.

• *A culture of openness.* Today's fast-paced world requires organizations to move quickly. Employees need to be able to challenge conventional wisdom. If messengers bearing bad news are routinely slain, the organization's leadership will hear only what it wants to hear, and failure will loom around the next corner.

- *Institutionalization of project management.* Project management needs to be practiced in a conscious fashion. It needs to gain explicit support from senior management. Its systematic pursuit should become openly embedded in the organization's goals. It needs to become a line item in the budget. Without this institutionalization of project management, projects are likely to be carried out in an accidental, ad hoc fashion.

Each of these items is discussed in more detail later in the chapter.

Approaches to Assessing Organizational Competence

There is nothing new in the idea that organizations should be reviewed to assess whether they meet some predetermined standards of operation. Restaurants, for example, must meet certain health standards before they are issued operating licenses by municipal governments. Travel agencies must demonstrate that they pursue good business practices before they are certified to issue airline tickets. Business schools must achieve certain operating standards before they are accredited by the American Assembly of Collegiate Schools of Business. In each case, some sort of assessment process is established for determining whether the organizations being reviewed meet a set of defined standards in doing their business.

The process of reviewing organizational performance and certifying that established standards are being achieved goes by various names, such as licensure, accreditation, or certification. Traditionally this review process has been applied in businesses where safety or health or fiduciary responsibilities are factors that must be reckoned with. In these cases, performance assessments are made to assure the public that their interests are being served.

What is interesting about the recent initiatives in the quality arena (the Deming Prize, the ISO 9000, the Baldrige award, and the CMM) is that they are being undertaken primarily to address the following question: Is our organization doing the best job possible in conducting its affairs? Thus the concern here is not with serving the public interest but rather with pushing the organization to meet or exceed industry "best practices." It is axiomatic that if industry standards are not being met, the organization is in trouble. At best it is performing suboptimally. At worst, it is flirting with bankruptcy.

Attempts to assess organizational competence in the project management arena are in their infancy. To date, no clearly defined and generally accepted assessment process has been developed, although various initiatives are under way in different quarters. As these initiatives are being pursued, it is clear that they are following an approach comparable to efforts to assess organizational performance in the quality arena. For example, Micro-Frame Technologies has developed a Project Management Maturity Model that closely parallels the CMM (Remy, 1997). Like the CMM, it identifies five levels of maturity that a project-based organization can achieve:

1. *Ad hoc:* Each project is viewed as unique and autonomous.
2. *Abbreviated:* Although project management tools are viewed as leading to improved performance, schedules are not derived as the consequence of disciplined planning methodologies.
3. *Organized:* A basic template is adopted that can apply to all projects.
4. *Managed:* A schedule methodology, data standards, and simplification of plans are stressed.
5. *Adaptive:* The majority of projects consistently employ conscious methodologies to schedule projects and manage project information.

This model is discussed in greater detail in Chapter Twelve.

A major player in the project management education and training arena—ESI—has, in conjunction with the consultant Ginger Levin, adopted its own maturity assessment model, which it calls ProjectFRAMEWORK (Levin, Ward, and Hill, 1998). This approach makes heavy use of internal and external assessors to evaluate the project management maturity level of an organization with a view to offering guidance on how to perform its operations.

Adesh Jain (1998) of the Centre for Excellence in Project Management in New Delhi has taken an entirely different approach to examining project management maturity. His levels are behaviorally focused: ad hoc, ritual, compulsive, leadership, visionary, and passion-based.

In the late 1990s, the Project Management Institute took steps to establish global standards in developing a project management maturity model (Duncan, 1998). Their approach is to bring together a large number of project professionals from a wide range of industries to review existing efforts at assessing project management competence at the organizational level and to work out uniform standards for such assessments.

The matter of assessing organizational competence for project-based organizations has even become the topic of a doctoral dissertation by Kenneth Stevenson (1998). This work appears to be the most comprehensive attempt to date to put project management organizational competence into the broader context of competency assessments as pursued by scholars and consultants over the past two decades.

At this time, then, a number of players have taken steps to get a handle on assessing project management competence at the organizational level. It should be noted, however, that although these efforts appear promising, no universally accepted approach to the matter has yet been developed.

This chapter offers a practical approach to examining organizational competence for project-based operations. It reviews the general steps that can be taken to assess organizational competence. The next chapter offers an organizational self-assessment checklist, as well as specific information on evaluation criteria being employed in two highly successful quality assessment processes: the ISO 9000 and the CMM. These two successful assessment models offer an idea of what needs to be done to carry out effective competency assessments in the project management arena.

General Steps in Assessing Organizational Competence

A review of current efforts to conduct organizational assessments across a variety of industries shows that these efforts typically entail a number of common features:

- *Adoption of performance standards.* Performance standards need to be developed and adopted. Target organizations are then evaluated against these standards. In mature industries (such as construction, defense, and pharmaceuticals), basic standards were developed long ago. Even these need to be adjusted regularly, however, to reflect changing conditions. In project management, a standard has been created to assess the knowledge-based competence of individuals (the *Guide to the Project Management Body of Knowledge* by Duncan, 1996, which was discussed in some detail in Chapter Four). No universally accepted standard for assessing organizational competence exists at this time, however.

• *Assessment of what it will take to achieve the standards.* This is often accomplished through self-study efforts in which a self-study assessment team examines organizational processes and structures to identify what steps need to be taken to enable the organization to achieve the desired performance standards.

• *Development of a plan that lays out the steps needed to achieve the standards.* Once the self-study team has identified what needs to be done to achieve the standards, a detailed plan should be created that shows in a step-by-step sequence what the organization should do.

• *Implementation of the plan.* Business processes must be reengineered in conformance with the plan. The organization may need to restructure its operations.

• *Implementation of the assessments to see whether the organization is meeting the standards.* The assessment often entails employing an EISA approach—external, internal, and self-assessment (Wilson and Pearson, 1995). First, a self-assessment is often conducted by people in the targeted work unit. They can develop a sense of whether the standards are being achieved. Then an independent set of auditors from within the organization conducts an internal assessment. Finally, external assessors working on behalf of the accrediting body are brought in to conduct a fully objective assessment of whether the work unit is in compliance with the standards.

• *Documentation of findings.* After conducting their audit, the external assessors write a report indicating the extent to which the targeted work unit is in compliance with the standards.

Key Elements of Organizational Competence in Project-Based Organizations

It was mentioned earlier that organizational competence is tied to the level of support that organizations provide their employees, enabling them to do the best job possible. There are seven key elements that lead to organizational competence in project management:

1. Clearly defined and well-formulated procedures for performing work
2. Access to information needed to perform work effectively
3. Sufficient quantities of qualified human and material resources
4. Opportunities for training and education
5. Clearly defined visions of where the organization is headed
6. A culture of openness
7. Institutionalization of project management

In general, organizations that perform well on these seven elements are likely to carry out their projects competently.

Each of the seven elements is discussed in detail.

Element 1: Clearly Defined and Well-Formulated Procedures for Performing Work

It is quite popular to bash bureaucracy these days. Public opinion polls show that in the United States the exemplar of bureaucracy—government—receives little respect from citizens. The collapse of the Soviet Union was closely tied to the bureaucratic excesses of its communist system. In China, which has maintained record-breaking growth levels for two decades, the weakest economic performance has come from state-owned (that is, excessively bureaucratic) enterprises. In Western economies, one of the key objectives of the business process reengineering fad has been to strip companies of bureaucratic encumbrances. Some management thinkers have proclaimed "the end of bureaucracy" (Pinchot and Pinchot, 1993). Lean operations are in, bloated bureaucracy is out.

Even as some thinkers are placing the ashes of bureaucracy into a historical sarcophagus, well-respected competency assessment models (such as the ISO 9000, the Deming Prize, the Baldrige Award, and the CMM) are defining competence in terms of adherence to well-formulated and consistently applied business processes. For example, much of the ISO 9000 approach to identifying high-quality organizations centers on studying whether they have clearly defined business processes that are consistently followed. The CMM maintains that organizations that lack well-defined business processes and that conduct their work in an ad hoc fashion are immature organizations. In fact, the CMM defines maturity in terms of mastery of business processes. What all this means is that at least some aspects of bureaucracy, which is driven by the definition and pursuit of clearly defined processes, are still recognized to possess value.

Few of us find bureaucracy appealing because we recognize that obsession with detail and rigid adherence to rules, which are common traits associated with the worst bureaucrats, do not lead to high performance. Most people today see bureaucracy as inherently dysfunctional. This view of bureaucracy is quite recent. Seminal writers such as Max Weber (1947), Thorsten Veblen (1915), and Joseph Schumpeter (1950) have recognized that the employment of bureaucratic processes enables organizations to cope with increasingly complex problems. It has been since only the 1970s and 1980s that bureaucracy has become anathema to large numbers of citizens and thinkers.

Clearly an important feature of competent organizations is that they have established intelligent, clear, and consistently applied procedures to guide the organization's work efforts. Any organization desiring to assess its project management competence should review the efficacy of its procedures. One useful approach to identifying what procedures should be emphasized is to examine procedures associated with different phases of a project's life cycle. Following is a list that suggests the types of procedures carried out in different project life-cycle phases:

Needs Assessment Phase

- Procedures for the systematic identification of stakeholders
- Procedures for the systematic review of stakeholders' needs (such as interviews, questionnaires, and focus group exercises)
- Procedures for managing changes to needs and requirements (such as configuration management)

Project Selection Phase

- Procedures for the development of proposals, feasibility studies, businesses cases, or competitive analyses

- Procedures for selecting projects through formal processes (such as benefit-cost ratio analysis, Murder Boards, project scoring sheets, and analytical hierarchy process)
- Procedures for negotiating and writing contracts to engage in project work
- Risk management procedures to ascertain whether promised dates, budgets, and resource allocations can be met, as defined by contractual obligations (such as use of Monte Carlo simulation, model building, and scenario building)
- Procedures for accepting or rejecting the terms and conditions written into contracts, before contracts are actually signed

Planning and Development Phase

- Procedures for developing clearly defined requirements
- Procedures for pursuing clearly defined development methodologies
- Procedures for planning budgets, schedules, and resource allocations (including competence in developing standard project management tools such as PERT charts, Gantt charts, S-curves, and resource histograms)

Implementation Phase

- Procedures for step-by-step implementation of solutions
- Procedures for generating and capturing project performance data
- Procedures for acquiring resources
- Procedures for structuring teams
- Procedures for rewarding and punishing project performance

Control Phase

- Procedures for tracking actual versus planned schedule, budget, resource, and technical performance
- Procedures for taking corrective action

Evaluation Phase

- Procedures for identifying competent internal and external evaluators

- Procedures for conducting periodic tests
- Procedures for conducting a wide array of evaluative activities, including preliminary design reviews, detailed design reviews, performance appraisal reviews, customer acceptance reviews, and management-by-objectives reviews
- Procedures for implementing recommendations of evaluative efforts

Closeout Phase

- Procedures for assembling project documentation
- Procedures for achieving customer acceptance
- Procedures for reallocating resources
- Procedures for handing over deliverables to customers
- Procedures for conducting postproject, lessons-learned exercises

Element 2: Access to Information Needed to Perform Work Effectively

Competent organizations have systems in place that provide individuals and teams with the information they need to carry out their work effectively. Without such information, team members are flying blind. They do not know what resources are available to do the job. They are ignorant of their budget status and they risk spending more money than is available. They are unable to answer urgent customer inquiries about the status of the project—and so on. It is difficult to perform competently if one is operating from ignorance.

For the needed information to be useful it should possess at least three traits. First, it should be accurate. The accuracy of data is closely tied to the adequacy of the data collection effort. If data are collected in an ad hoc fashion, it is unlikely to be accurate ("Hey, George, how long do you think it will take to install this piece of equipment?" hardly reflects an adequate data collection methodology). Some of the data collection tools commonly employed in project management consistently generate questionable information. For example, an informal study I carried out a few years ago on the adequacy of time sheet data suggests that they offer highly imperfect information on how people spend their time on projects.

Second, the information should be timely. For example, a common complaint about the budget data supplied to project workers is that information on expenditures is reported too late, say, four to six weeks after the expenditure has been made. With this kind of lag in reporting data, team members are uncertain of their exact budget status. What organizations should strive for is to provide teams with real-time access to needed data. In an ideal world, project workers should be able to tap into the corporate database and determine, say, budget status on the project as of midnight of the previous day.

Finally, the information should be readily accessible. Whether the data are supplied in a hard-copy format or by means of computerized searches, project workers should be able to access them easily. If access becomes too difficult because the data query system is excessively complex, then a major barrier to acquiring needed information has been created. In such a situation the data do not really exist for all intents and purposes.

Specific categories of data that should be available to project workers in competent organizations include the following:

• *Budget data.* An important requirement here is that the budget data be activity based. Today many organizations are developing activity-based-costing accounting systems to enable them to track project costs. These are commonly known as ABC accounting systems.

• *Order processing data.* Project team members, sales staff, and customers are all interested in knowing the status of an order at any given moment. Can they get this information?

• *Schedule data.* Today time is the "killer constraint." Project team members must know the schedule status of their projects so they can determine whether they can meet their promised delivery dates.

• *Data on human and material resource availability.* During the planning phase of a project, planners must have a good sense of what human and material resources are available to work on the project. As the project is being carried out and encounters schedule slippages, this type of information is crucial for identifying what resources can be accessed to bring the project back on schedule.

• *Inventory data.* On projects that depend heavily on the use of stockpiled materials it is important to know whether inventory levels are adequate and whether new materials should be ordered to replenish the stocks.

• *Historical data on past project performance.* During the project selection and planning phases, it is important to have historical data available on schedule, budget, and resource performance for previous projects in order to generate accurate estimates for future projects.

Element 3: Sufficient Quantities of Qualified Human and Material Resources

Effective project work requires that the project team be able to acquire the right resources at the right time. It is important to recognize that the timing of resource allocations is as important as the quality of resources employed. (Having Albert Einstein assigned to my team is not very helpful if Dr. Einstein is brought in a week too early or a week too late.) The most competent organizations create environments that ensure that resource bottlenecks do not create problems.

For this element to be satisfied, two conditions must be met. First, adequate quantities of qualified resources must exist. Obviously if it takes three people to carry out a particular task in two days, then anything short of three people will create problems. Either the workers will have to work longer days, management will have to accept that the task will encounter a schedule slippage, or the specifications for the task will need to be scaled back.

Traditionally when organizations thought of the availability of resources, they focused on resources employed by the organization. With the recent emphasis on outsourcing (that is, contracting out work to outsiders), organizations have dramatically increased their flexibility in acquiring the needed resources. Even so, however, they can encounter bottlenecks as they find it difficult to identify capable contractors who can supply the needed resources at the right time.

Second, processes must exist to enable resources to be allocated effectively. Part of the horror of the famines in the Horn of Africa in the 1990s was the realization that although adequate stores of food existed, people were starving because of difficulties in distributing the food because of warfare in the region. So it is with project resources: an organization can have an abundance of qualified resources, but are they being allocated to the right places at the right time?

Element 4: Opportunities for Training and Education

Much has been said in recent years about the need for continual learning in today's rapidly changing world. Education never stops. This is true for individuals and organizations alike. Individual men and women must be committed to the constant upgrading of their skills and insights. Organizations must continually adapt to the new circumstances they face, just as biological organisms adapt to changes in their environments.

The most competent organizations provide their employees with an abundance of learning opportunities. These opportunities come in a variety of packages. For example, organizations can pay some or all of the tuition for employees enrolled in university courses. They can supply needed training through their internal training departments, or they can enable employees to be trained by outside trainers. They can make mentors available to give workers on-the-spot guidance when needed. They can emphasize on-the-job learning experiences, taking a learning-by-doing perspective. Most important, they can create an environment in which workers crave to learn.

This last point is significant, because even the most enlightened organizations will not be able to offer all the training and education their employees need. As I stated in Chapter Five in my discussion of the need for personal mastery, workers themselves will have to assume responsibility for learning much of what they need to know. If they need to develop computer spreadsheet skills, then hopefully they will make it their business to learn how to use spreadsheets, by hook or by crook!

Element 5: Clearly Defined Visions of Where the Organization Is Headed

In the early 1990s, one of the most visible management crazes was the move to create organizational mission and vision statements. The theory was that if managers and workers had a full grasp of what their organizations were about, if they understood the culture in which they operated, and if they perceived the direction being taken by the organization at a high conceptual level, this understanding would drive all of the organization's operations from top to bottom. It became an article of faith that in organizations where managers and employees do not understand the organization's mission and vision, the organization is in some sense adrift.

I think that the general theory behind this perspective is on target. In large measure an organization's coherence is closely tied to the clarity of its mission and vision. Well-formulated and understood missions and visions provide the basic drumbeat that gets everyone marching together. This idea corresponds to the idea of building a shared vision, identified by Senge (1990) as one of five key disciplines that effective organizations must pursue.

Where the mission-and-vision movement went awry was in its implementation. I participated in several undertakings to formulate mission and vision statements and developed a sense that they were well meaning but slightly ludicrous exercises. In each case, clusters of managers would be divided into various small teams that would tackle different aspects of the mission-vision issue. Typically they would hover around a flip chart, fill out a large page with their insights, tear the page off the flip chart, and attach it to a wall. They would then turn to a fresh page and begin the process again. Periodically the teams would stop their work and a plenary session would be held in which an attempt would be made to aggregate the views of the separate teams. Heavy use would be made of Post-it Notes and sticky buttons at this point. Enormous time would be dedicated to collective wordsmithing. Quite often the people with the weakest grammatical skills would dominate the discussion. At the end of two or three days of this type of activity, mission and vision statements would emerge, the participants would return home, and the organization would continue to operate in a business-as-usual fashion. When the mission and vision statements were finally proclaimed to the workers at large, the announcements would often be met with knowing smirks from the rank and file. When all is said and done, little was truly accomplished through this elaborate exercise.

Still, it is important for the organization to have an established vision and for its employees to possess a strong sense of the organization's mission. Not only does this provide the organization's efforts with a focus, but it also energizes the workforce, converting them into inspired, hard-driving "missionaries." I suspect that well-formulated mission and vision statements are achieved by exercising effective leadership rather than by convening mission and vision work groups. A defining characteristic of all great leaders in history has been their ability to convey a shared vision to their followers. Competent organizations need visionary leaders!

Element 6: A Culture of Openness

In an organization if messengers who bear bad news are killed, it is impossible for the organization to operate competently. Effective management is heavily dependent on access to accurate and timely data. Anything that blocks the flow of information or that encourages its distortion contributes to suboptimal performance at best and serious organizational pathologies at worst.

The need for a culture of openness in conducting an enterprise's affairs is universally accepted in theory. Today's most competent organizations are pursuing cultures of openness because it makes good business sense, not because they are operating according to altruistic motivations. Policies that promote openness—such as employee empowerment policies, 360-degree evaluations, open-door policies, and suggestion boxes—enable organizations to be more responsive to stakeholders' needs and wants. Such policies increase the likelihood that problems are not buried but are surfaced early so they can be dealt with while they are still manageable. Such policies enable organizations to operate quickly and nimbly.

One of the best-articulated statements of the compelling need for openness was presented by a colleague of mine, William E. Halal, while I was at George Washington University. In *The New Management* (1996), Halal argues convincingly that to survive today's competitive pressures, organizations are being forced to base their operations on the twin pillars of *enterprise* and *democracy*. Both of these approaches demand an environment of openness. The new focus on enterprise means that work units within organizations must operate like independent businesses. They must have a strong market focus. What is interesting is that work units' concern for *internal* markets (markets within the organization) should be as strong as their concern for traditional *external* markets. To operate like businesses, these work units must be given a strong measure of decision-making authority that was unthinkable in traditional hierarchical organizations. To operate democratically, they must function in a collaborative fashion with all the stakeholders affected by their activities, including their customers and vendors.

Any worthwhile review of organizational competence in project management should assess the extent to which the target organization supports a culture of openness. Are channels open that enable the free-flow communication of information among members of the organization's community? Do workers have access to the gamut of information needed to do their jobs (including financial and production information that might have been treated confidentially in the past)? Does the organization's culture encourage the give and take of ideas? Is criticism of the establishment permitted? Are there taboos (topics that cannot be broached because they are heretical)? Are employees empowered to make meaningful decisions that affect their performance? And so on.

Element 7: Institutionalization of Project Management

For an organization to be competent in implementing projects, it cannot treat project management casually. For decades project management has been labeled "the accidental profession," reflecting the fact that people often become project managers by accident, and once they do they learn their jobs through trial and error—that is to say, by accident. As organizations turn their attention to carrying out their efforts through projects, they must deal with project management consciously and systematically. That is, they must institutionalize it.

Institutionalization may be as simple as developing a set of project management methods and procedures, writing and distributing a project management handbook, or establishing standards for purchasing project management software. This ad hoc approach to incorporating project management into the organization may work when project activity is meager, but as projects assume a more significant role in the organization's efforts, a more formal approach is needed.

Today the institutionalization of project management often entails establishing a project office. At the time of this writing, the creation of project offices in both business and government enterprises is growing exponentially. There are a variety of functions that these offices can carry out, but it is clear that they are beginning to assume a common modus operandi. My book *Project Office: A Key to Managing Projects Effectively,* coauthored with Tom Block (1997), describes five fairly standard types of project office activities:

- *Provide the organization with project administrative support.* Project office staff can maintain project schedules and budgets, identify resource availability, help maintain time sheets, and undertake other activities of this type.

- *Offer project management consulting and mentoring services to the organization.* The majority of most organizations' employees are unfamiliar with project management principles, and regrettably top management is often included among the ranks of the uninitiated. Project offices can supply different internal players with consultants who can assist in performing project-related activities, such as writing a proposal, developing a work breakdown structure, or implementing a PERT/CPM scheduling network. Beyond this, project offices can offer the services of project mentors, who can work shoulder to shoulder with employees, showing them how to execute project work effectively.

- *Develop and maintain project management standards and methods.* One of the primary responsibilities of a project office is the development and maintenance of standards and methods that will enable projects to be carried out in a rational and consistent fashion. For example, most project offices identify standards for the employment of scheduling, database, spreadsheet, and graphics software. They also create forms that project teams can use to guide their management efforts. They promulgate important management methods in the areas of project selection, evaluation, change control, and risk assessment.

- *Provide project management training.* Project office staff often work closely with the organization's training department to supply pertinent project management training to employees. They identify what the training needs are and suggest the types of courses that address those needs. They may be actively involved in course development. They may even supply instructors for some courses. If the organization depends on outside vendors to supply the training needs, the project office plays a role in identifying capable vendors and working with them to ensure that the course offerings are relevant to the organization's specific requirements.

• *Supply the organization with project managers.* As project offices grow in size, they may become the home for the organization's cadre of project managers. In this case, when a new project is launched, project office staff identify a project manager who is best suited to head the effort. They also assume responsibility for the professional development of the organization's project managers by coaching them on career moves, identifying areas in which they need to strengthen their skills, and evaluating their work efforts.

Conclusions

On projects of any complexity it is not enough simply to assemble smart people into teams to get the job done. For individuals and teams to function effectively, they must receive the support they need from their organizations. This support may be manifested physically (such as in up-to-date equipment and good accounting systems) or socially (such as in emotional backing from senior management and free and open communications). The point is that low levels of support can undermine the best efforts of capable people and cohesive teams.

The competence of organizations is rooted in their ability to support their people, both as individuals and teams. Thus any attempt at assessing organizational competence should focus on this point.

Current attempts to measure organizational competence in the project management arena borrow heavily from assessment approaches employed by the quality management community. These approaches have organizational work units undergo external assessments, internal assessments, and self-assessments. It is hoped that the successes that the quality management community has achieved in assessing the quality effectiveness of organizations can be repeated in the project management arena.

Chapter Twelve

Assessing Organizational Competence

An obvious question that many readers may have at this point is, How do I determine how competent my organization is in the implementation of its projects? Given the absence of a well-established, systematic assessment methodology—such as the approaches taken by the ISO 9000, the Capability Maturity Model (CMM), the Deming Prize, or the Baldrige Award—organizations cannot simply turn to written guidelines or solicit insights from an expert who has carried out such assessments before. I suspect that the best organizations can do is adopt a fairly unstructured approach to the issue. If the competency assessment is an important part of a reengineering exercise, the organization may want to employ a full-blown external, internal, self-assessment (EISA) review. If it is simply a "sanity check," then a small working group may be assembled to examine the organization's capabilities using a checklist approach.

Whatever specific criteria are employed in the assessment, they should address the seven broad assessment questions discussed in this chapter:

1. Do we have clearly defined and well-established procedures in place for carrying out our project work?
2. Do we have information systems in place that will offer our project workers access to the information they need to do a good job?
3. Do we consistently acquire sufficient quantities of qualified human and material resources to carry out our project work?

4. Are the workers we depend on able to obtain the education and training they need to operate effectively?
5. Do we have a clear sense of what our organization's core goals are and where it is headed?
6. Has a milieu of openness been established in our organization?
7. Has project management been institutionalized in the organization?

Each of these questions should be answered with a hearty yes. When the organization understands that its competence is based on its capacity to support project efforts, it will realize that the more noes it utters in answering these questions, the less competent it is.

Specific Approaches to Assessing Organizational Competence: The ISO 9000 and the CMM

Two heavily used approaches to assessing organizational competence are the ISO 9000 approach, which is used to determine the extent to which an organization's business processes support the production of high-quality goods, and the CMM approach, which examines the extent to which information technology (IT) work units have achieved "maturity" in managing IT work efforts. The purpose of this review is to illustrate key features of these enormously successful approaches to assaying organizational competence. As the attempt is made to develop an organizational competency model for project management, the principal traits that have enabled the ISO 9000 and the CMM approaches to function so effectively should be kept in mind.

The ISO 9000 Approach to Assessing Organizational Competence

The International Organization for Standards established ISO 9000 as a mechanism for enabling organizations to determine the degree to which their business processes promote the production of high-quality goods and services.

An organization that wishes to achieve ISO 9000 certification goes through a period of self-study and preparation, during which it strengthens its business processes. Then a team of ISO-approved auditors reviews the organization's processes and determines whether these processes are in compliance with a number of pre-established criteria. If the auditors find that compliance has been achieved, the organization is certified as being ISO 9000 compliant.

ISO 9000 certification carries with it a number of clear benefits. For example, companies desiring to do business in Europe (or in places such as Singapore) must give serious consideration to being certified, because the members of the European Union require it. Beyond this, the very act of preparing for an ISO 9000 audit forces senior managers in companies to take quality improvement seriously, because if the audit team senses a lack of senior management support in this area, it is grounds for denying certification.

An interesting feature of the ISO 9000 approach is that *it does not certify that an organization is producing high-quality goods and services*. Rather, it certifies that an organization has processes in place that are clearly defined and consistently applied and that in the final analysis can lead to the production of high-quality goods and services. Thus there is no guarantee that a specific product built at an ISO 9000 certified organization is of high quality. Some critics suggest that it is entirely possible that a company with clearly defined and consistently applied processes can achieve ISO 9000 certification even though it produces mediocre products.

Although there is merit in this criticism, the focus on validating processes (rather than on tangible products) can be supported on both theoretical and practical grounds. Theoretically, a requirement for the production of high-quality products is the consistent application of clearly defined processes. You do not get high-quality goods by doing your job haphazardly! So the focus on processes has merit on theoretical grounds.

Practically speaking, it is far easier to assess whether an organization has clearly defined processes that are being carried out consistently than it is to determine whether the goods and services it produces are of high quality according to some objective measure. Objective measures of quality are notoriously evanescent. Just because a good is highly priced does not mean it is of high quality. Just because it incorporates the most advanced technology does not mean it is of high quality. Just because it operates without breaking down does not mean it is of high quality.

What then constitutes a high-quality product? The ISO 9000 perspective holds that quality is basically what customers *perceive* it to be. There is no attempt to measure quality according to an objective standard. Although this view may seem illogical at first blush, careful reflection suggests that it makes sense. In the final analysis, those who use a good or service are in the best position to assess its merits. To them, the key question is, Does this good or service meet my needs and wants? Built into the answer are presumptions of product reliability (most certainly, unreliable goods and services do not meet the needs and wants of normal customers). Beyond this, the definition takes into account the matter of usability: goods that are placed on the shelf unused cannot be viewed as possessing high quality, no matter how sophisticated and reliable they are.

The ISO 9000 approach certifies the adequacy of business processes at three levels, reflected in three ISO 9000 documents (ISO 9001, ISO 9002, and ISO 9003). ISO 9001 has the broadest scope. The processes of organizations undergoing a 9001 assessment are reviewed according to twenty "quality elements." These elements in turn fall into five categories: design and development, procurement, production, installation, and servicing.

Organizations achieving ISO 9001 certification are full-service organizations engaged in cradle-to-grave business activity. Organizations with more limited activity can opt for 9002 or 9003 certification. ISO 9002 reviews eighteen quality elements in the areas of procurement, production, and installation, while ISO 9003 focuses on twelve quality elements in the area of production.

The CMM Approach to Assessing Organizational Competence

The CMM was developed at Carnegie Mellon University's Software Engineering Institute (SEI). It recognizes that there are wide variations in the maturity of organizations to manage their software development efforts. In most organizations, the software management process is ad hoc, reflecting a low level of maturity. Few processes are defined and success is often the product of the heroic efforts of individuals. In the most capable organizations, the process is repeatable and fully under control, reflecting a high level of maturity.

The CMM approach attempts to assess an organization's level of software maturity in accordance with preestablished criteria. Maturity is divided into five levels (Software Engineering Institute, 1993a):

Level 1: Initial. The software process is ad hoc, occasionally chaotic. Few processes are defined, and success depends on individual effort and heroics. Key process areas: none.

Level 2: Repeatable. Basic project management processes are established to track cost, schedule, and functionality. A process discipline is in place to repeat earlier successes with similar applications. Key process areas are as follows:

- Requirements management
- Software project planning
- Software project tracking and oversight
- Software subcontract management
- Software quality assurance
- Software configuration management

Level 3: Defined. The software process for both management and engineering activities is documented, standardized, and integrated into a standard software process for the organization. All projects use an approved, tailored version of the organization's standard software process for developing and maintaining software. Key process areas are as follows:

- Organization process focus
- Organization process definition
- Training program
- Integrated software management
- Software product engineering
- Intergroup coordination
- Peer reviews

Level 4: Managed. Detailed measures of the software process and products are quantitatively understood and controlled. Key process areas are as follows:

- Quantitative process management
- Software quality management

Level 5: Optimizing. Continuous process improvement is enabled by quantitative feedback from the process and from piloting innovative ideas and technologies. Key process areas are as follows:

- Defect prevention
- Technology change management
- Process change management

Each of these key process areas is in turn assessed according to five "common features" (Software Engineering Institute, 1993b). These are as follows:

- *Commitment to perform:* Are actions being taken to ensure that the process is established and that it will endure (such as establishing policies and senior sponsorship)?
- *Ability to perform:* Are the proper resources, organizational structures, and training available?
- *Activities performed:* Are plans and procedures established, work performed and tracked, and necessary corrective actions taken?
- *Measurement and analysis:* Have measures and procedures been developed to analyze status and effectiveness of the activities performed?
- *Verifying implementation:* Have reviews and audits been performed to ensure that work is being accomplished using established procedures?

The actual assessment effort entails four steps. First, a team of CMM-approved assessors is identified. These assessors guide the assessment process. Second, a detailed maturity questionnaire is filled out by the target organization. The assessment team reviews the filled-out questionnaire to identify strengths and deficiencies in the target organization. Third, the assessment team carries out a site visit (typically for five days). During this visit they have an opportunity to view the target organization's processes firsthand. Finally, as a consequence of their investigations, the members of the assessment team generate findings detailing the strengths and weaknesses of the software process at the target organization.

Conclusions

A review of the ISO 9000 and CMM approaches offers several lessons for anyone wishing to implement a process to assess organizational competence. One lesson is that the process that is implemented needs to focus on the achievement of carefully thought out, predetermined standards. Otherwise, organizations operate in an ad hoc manner, defining their performance according to moment-by-moment exigencies. Researchers at the SEI have found that most software organizations function this way (approximately 80 percent). Chances are that the software experience can be extrapolated to many other industries.

The key question now is, What set of standards should be adopted to define organizational competence in the project management arena? As introduced in Chapter Eleven, one consulting company has reported developing a project management maturity model that borrows heavily from the CMM (Remy, 1997). As with the CMM, this model identifies five levels of maturity (that is, competence):

1. *Ad hoc:* Each project is viewed as unique and autonomous. Little or no use is made of historical data on project performance.
2. *Abbreviated:* Although the first attempts are made to introduce a project management discipline in performing project work, the efforts are rather haphazard. For example, some projects may be scheduled with too much detail while others employ insufficient data.
3. *Organized:* Scope development is carried out carefully. Use is made of historical experience. Project planning is based on models, and scheduling and budgeting exercises must be reconciled with them.
4. *Managed:* Historical experience is used to update models and data sets regularly. Key data elements and templates are standardized. Forecasting is performed using a consolidated database.
5. *Adaptive:* The historical project archive is on-line and continually updated. Modeling enables data to be maintained at fine levels of detail. Modules can be pasted together, enabling the

flexible use of project models. Integrated cost-schedule-resource analyses can be carried out at the enterprise level as well as at the project level.

Beyond this, the management of projects is divided into eight major sections, and these sections are then broken down into a total of fifty-one categories. The eight sections are as follows:

- *Leadership and management:* Focus is on human factors and the cultural environment in which project work is carried out.
- *Project performance management:* Focus is on the management and control of individual projects within a multiproject organization.
- *Problem-risk-opportunity management:* Focus is on a structured approach to identifying risks and opportunities and mitigating risk.
- *Multiproject management system:* Focus is on identifying and understanding the institutional framework of project management within the organization.
- *Management information:* Focus is on the kind and flow of data employed throughout the multiproject organization.
- *Policies and procedures:* Focus is on the documentation used to get the job done.
- *Data management:* Focus is on the standards for developing, accessing, and maintaining project management data.
- *Education and training:* Focus is on the extent to which workers are given the opportunity to gain new insights and to improve their skills through education and training.

Organizational Self-Assessment Checklist

The following assessment checklist examines the project competence of organizations according to a number of functions that effective project-based organizations should be able to achieve. The checklist can be used to identify the overall degree of organizational competence. It can also be employed as a diagnostic tool to identify general organizational strengths and weaknesses.

The assessment checklist can be filled out by any number of players. Following the EISA procedure, the checklist can be filled out by external reviewers, internal reviewers, self-assessors, or any combination of the three. Scores should be tabulated for each item. There are a total of 61 items in the form, so a total score of less than 183 (61 items × score of 3, indicating adequate performance) indicates a team that is performing in a less-than-adequate fashion overall. Beyond this aggregate view, any item with a score of 2 or less represents a trouble spot, contributing to low levels of organizational performance. All items with a score of 2 or less should be highlighted and corrective action should be taken to deal with them.

Scoring Key

1 and 2 = inadequate

3 = just adequate

4 and 5 = more than adequate

1. Do we have clearly defined and well-established procedures in place for carrying out our project work?

Item: Needs Assessment Phase		*Score*
Clarity of overall mission of the team effort	1 2 3 4 5	__
Procedures for the systematic identification of stakeholders	1 2 3 4 5	__
Procedures for the systematic review of stakeholders' needs (such as interviews, questionnaires, and focus group exercises)	1 2 3 4 5	__
Procedures for managing changes to needs and requirements (such as configuration management)	1 2 3 4 5	__
Total		__

Item: Project Selection Phase		*Score*
Procedures for the development of proposals, feasibility studies, business cases, or competitive analyses	1 2 3 4 5	__

Procedures for selecting projects using formal
processes such as benefit-cost analysis or
Murder Boards   1 2 3 4 5   __

Procedures for negotiating and writing
contracts to engage in project work   1 2 3 4 5   __

Risk management procedures to ascertain
whether promised dates, budgets, and
resource allocations can be met (for example,
using Monte Carlo simulation)   1 2 3 4 5   __

Procedures for accepting or rejecting the
terms and conditions for project work before
contracts are signed   1 2 3 4 5   __

Total   __

Item: Planning and Development Phase   *Score*

Procedures for developing clearly defined
requirements   1 2 3 4 5   __

Use of established scheduling tools for
planning purposes (such as Gantt charts
and PERT/CPM charts)   1 2 3 4 5   __

Use of sound cost data for budgeting purposes   1 2 3 4 5   __

Use of systematic cost-estimating procedures   1 2 3 4 5   __

Use of systematic resource allocation
techniques   1 2 3 4 5   __

Total   __

Item: Implementation Phase   *Score*

Procedures for step-by-step implementation
of solutions   1 2 3 4 5   __

Procedures for generating and capturing
project performance data   1 2 3 4 5   __

Procedures for acquiring resources
systematically   1 2 3 4 5   __

Explicit procedures for structuring project
teams   1 2 3 4 5   __

Procedures for rewarding and punishing
project performance   1 2 3 4 5   __

Total   __

Item: Control Phase   Score

Procedures for tracking actual versus
planned schedules, budgets, resources,
and technical performance   1 2 3 4 5   __
Procedures for taking corrective action
when variances grow large   1 2 3 4 5   __
Total   __

Item: Evaluation Phase   Score

Procedures for identifying competent
internal and external evaluators   1 2 3 4 5   __
Procedures for conducting periodic tests   1 2 3 4 5   __
Procedures for conducting a wide array of
evaluative activity (such as structured
walk-through, preliminary design reviews,
MBO reviews)   1 2 3 4 5   __
Procedures for implementing
recommendations of evaluative efforts   1 2 3 4 5   __
Total   __

Item: Closeout Phase   Score

Procedures for assembling project
documentation   1 2 3 4 5   __
Procedures for achieving customer
acceptance   1 2 3 4 5   __
Procedures for reallocating resources   1 2 3 4 5   __
Procedures for handing over deliverable
in an organized fashion   1 2 3 4 5   __
Procedures for conducting postproject
lessons-learned exercises   1 2 3 4 5   __
Total   __

2. Do we have information systems in place that will offer our project workers access to the information they need to do a good job?

Item   Score

In general, data that are accessed are timely   1 2 3 4 5   __
In general, data that are accessed are accurate 1 2 3 4 5   __

Access to useful schedule data	1 2 3 4 5	__
Access to useful budget data	1 2 3 4 5	__
Access to data on availability and use of human resources	1 2 3 4 5	__
Access to data on availability and use of material resources	1 2 3 4 5	__
Access to order-processing data	1 2 3 4 5	__
Access to inventory data	1 2 3 4 5	__
Access to historical data on performance of past projects	1 2 3 4 5	__
Total		__

3. Do we consistently acquire sufficient quantities of qualified human and material resources to carry out our project work?

Item		*Score*
Systematic approaches exist for acquiring human and material resources	1 2 3 4 5	__
Adequate quantities of human and material resources can be acquired consistently (both from within the organization and through outsourcing)	1 2 3 4 5	__
Resources can consistently be acquired in a timely fashion	1 2 3 4 5	__
Once resource commitments are made, they are kept	1 2 3 4 5	__
Total		__

4. Are the workers we depend on able to obtain the education and training they need to operate effectively?

Item		*Score*
The organization pays some or all of university-level course expenses	1 2 3 4 5	__
The organization provides workers on project teams with good training opportunities (such as ten days or more of formal training each year)	1 2 3 4 5	__

The organization offers mentoring
opportunities to those who need to develop
better job-related skills and insights   1 2 3 4 5   __
The organization supports a strong learning
environment   1 2 3 4 5   __
Total   __

5. Do we have a clear sense of what our organization's core goals are and where it is headed?

Item		Score
The organization has a clearly defined vision	1 2 3 4 5	__
Employees have a clear understanding of the organization's vision	1 2 3 4 5	__
The organization's processes and culture emphasize the establishment of clear goals on projects	1 2 3 4 5	__
Total		__

6. Has a milieu of openness been established in our organization?

Item		Score
Are communication channels open that enable the free flow of information among members of the organization's community?	1 2 3 4 5	__
Do project workers have access to the gamut of information needed to do their jobs, including financial and production information that might have been treated confidentially in the past?	1 2 3 4 5	__
Does the organization's culture encourage the give and take of ideas?	1 2 3 4 5	__
Is criticism of the establishment permitted?	1 2 3 4 5	__
Are there taboos (topics that cannot be broached because they are considered heretical)?	1 2 3 4 5	__

Are employees empowered to make
meaningful decisions that affect their
performance?   1 2 3 4 5   __
Total   __

7. Has project management been institutionalized in the organization?

Item	Score
The organization has clearly established methods and procedures for conducting projects that apply across the organization	1 2 3 4 5 __
The organization has a centralized project management information system	1 2 3 4 5 __
The organization has a clearly defined project management training curriculum	1 2 3 4 5 __
The organization has a project management handbook that is readily accessible to project staff and other pertinent personnel	1 2 3 4 5 __
The organization has established a project office	1 2 3 4 5 __
Total	__

Grand Total Score   __

Chapter Thirteen

Conclusion
Arriving at Competence

In thinking about what it takes to build a project-competent organization, it is helpful to go back once again to the Latin origins of the word *competence (competere)* which means to strive together. Project-competent organizations exist only when a whole range of players do their parts—when they strive together—to make competence happen.

Individual workers must be willing and able to learn. This entails a lot of work. Some of the learning must be directly job-related, while other learning must be broader. In part, workers must acquire knowledge and understanding through formal means and study. One does not just "pick up" techniques like Monte Carlo simulation. To learn Monte Carlo simulation, it is helpful to study it in a classroom setting with qualified instructors who can share their insights on the origins of the technique, its statistical roots, and how it can be applied most effectively. Then, after class, students must crack the books. For each hour of classroom instruction, competent students should spend three to five hours reviewing the material on their own.

But workers must also acquire knowledge and understanding through more informal processes. They should view their job sites as learning laboratories. For example, they should strive to achieve an understanding of what their colleagues are doing. They can do this by asking questions and observing their colleagues in action. In a sense all colleagues can be viewed as mentors, individuals who can coach them and provide them with insights that they would not acquire on their own. Employees should also work mightily to keep up with current events. What are the hot technologies making their way into offices these days? What are their counterparts doing in competing organizations?

Team members should work together to achieve agreed-upon performance objectives. They must recognize that there is more to teamwork than having team members feel good about one another. Effective teams are disciplined. Team members participate in required meetings, even when this is tedious, and they take seriously the demands to supply needed documentation. They are willing to suppress their egos in order to achieve the team's performance objectives. They recognize that their value to the team is tied to their competence, so they continually strive to improve their skills and knowledge.

Higher levels of management should do everything possible to create an environment that enables their employees to shine. The key word here is *support*. It is important that senior management offer their organizations both physical and moral support. By physical support I mean that they should supply the resources needed to enable their project workers to do their jobs effectively. For example, have they enabled their accounting systems to migrate from traditional general-ledger-based approaches to activity-based-costing approaches? Without activity-based accounting data, it is hard to see how project teams can be expected to be financially accountable for their actions. Has senior management done whatever is necessary to ensure that their project teams have up-to-date tools in the arenas of information and telecommunications technology? If their employees are operating in the information Stone Age, it is difficult to see how they can compete effectively against their colleagues who have access to current technology.

Moral support means that management creates a culture that encourages employees to excel in their tasks. High performance is encouraged, and slacking off is seen as unattractive. One way to create a healthy environment is to empower employees to make a wide array of decisions. By being part of the decision-making process, employees incur an obligation to perform their tasks effectively. This is the essence of ownership.

The Competence Dilemma Revisited

In Chapter One I briefly discussed what I call the *competence dilemma*. To restate the dilemma, it is recognizing that even while organizations purport to believe that, given the chance, everyone is capable of doing a good job, many people (perhaps the majority) simply *will not* or *cannot* rise to many of the challenges they encounter. For example, a significant problem may arise at work on a Friday afternoon. The tendency of most people would be to enjoy the weekend and deal with the problem Monday morning. In this instance, there is no compelling drive to deal effectively with important issues. Here we see individuals lacking the *will* to operate competently.

Another example: I recently observed an automobile accident in my community. Three cars were involved, and passengers in two of the cars were injured. A rookie policewoman arrived on the scene soon after the accident. She began to direct traffic in the area because a traffic jam was developing. She directed a car into oncoming traffic and another smashup occurred. To avoid a second pileup, the driver of another oncoming car swerved and hit one of the cars involved in the original accident. Its passenger, who had been injured in the original accident, was now thrown into the windshield and knocked unconscious. As mayhem ensued, the rookie policewoman was running from place to place, issuing orders that exacerbated the chaos. Thanks to her incompetence, a total of eight cars were drawn into the fray and five people were hospitalized. In this case, we encounter an individual who, though well intentioned, simply lacked the capability to do a good job.

There's really no great mystery here. Anyone who has attempted to hire someone to fill a job slot has experienced firsthand the reality that *there are enormous variations in people's capacity to do work*. I clearly recall my first attempt to hire a new employee back in the early 1970s. My company was looking for an entry-level research assistant with good writing and analytical skills. We placed an ad in the newspaper and received more than one hundred responses to it. Through a screening process we identified seven candidates we wanted to interview. My impression from their resumes was that they were all equally capable. They almost appeared to be clones. They all stated a desire to assume increased responsibilities on the job. They had all graduated from reputable universities with good grades. They had all majored in technical areas but had also taken a fair number of liberal arts courses—and so on.

What a shock I experienced once the interviews began. The first candidate we interviewed was a man who was under five feet tall and a semiprofessional weight lifter. His biceps were so big they almost tore open his jacket sleeves. He told us during the interview that he did not think he was qualified for the job and he indicated that he was not sure why he had responded to our ad. The next candidate was a tall, skinny woman who had some good analytical capabilities but could not write a grammatically correct sentence in the English language. And so it went. Remember, these two candidates were among those who had appeared most attractive during the first review of resumes. Although the resumes suggested a homogenous offering of job candidates, reality reflected an astonishing diversity.

To complicate matters, there does not appear to be a strong correlation between a person's track record in one area and his or her abilities in another. For example, I recently encountered a situation in which a marketing person who was able to generate $35 million of business in one company was hired and paid a high salary to generate business in another and utterly failed to generate a penny. He was then hired and paid a generous salary by a third company, and again he failed. A review of his situation showed that in the first company he had been fundamentally an order taker. His colleagues would set up contacts with important clients and he proved to be a genius at following up on the leads. In the two other companies, however, he was expected to generate leads himself, and this he could not do. Consequently he failed.

So, how to deal with the competence dilemma?

First, organizations must recognize that not all people are equally capable of doing a given job, *even when they are supported to the maximum extent.* This is such an obvious point that it should not be necessary to state it. However, so much of common wisdom and management literature is premised on the following proposition: Given the right levels of support, empowerment, and encouragement, nearly all people have the capacity to excel. This proposition simply does not hold up on Planet Earth! If, however, the sentence is adjusted in the following way, I think it is supportable: Given the right levels of support, empowerment, and encouragement, nearly all *highly competent people* have the capacity to excel.

Competence is rooted in a variety of factors, including motivation, energy, intelligence, skill level, and knowledge. Some people are highly motivated, others are not. Some possess an abundance of energy, others are lethargic. Some grasp the implications of issues in several nanoseconds, others remain clueless after three days of intense study. People are not programmed robots, and each person displays strong idiosyncratic elements.

Second, in dealing with people organizations must follow advice provided decades ago by Peter Drucker (1967), and that is to build on people's strengths. This means designing work to fit the worker. If a wood-carver, for instance, shows a special knack for taking advantage of the flow of the grain in red lancewood, let her work predominantly with red lancewood.

The greatest disappointments arise when organizations attempt to force workers to fit the job description. The ideal candidate for a job might be someone who is computer literate, has good writing skills, is self-starting, is statistically literate, is sensitive to customer issues, and possesses a sound knowledge of current events. These traits become the basis of a job description. Yet organizations generally find after extensive interviewing that no one candidate meets all the requirements. One or two may meet most of them, and ultimately one of these people is hired with a view to strengthening his or her weaknesses through training and job-related experience. Too often, however, the weaknesses continue to be weaknesses, and disappointment is expressed about the new worker's lack of competence.

Third, organizations should never forget that competence exists at three levels: the individual, the team, and the organization. True competence in its fullest sense is experienced only when these three levels are properly aligned. That is, capable people do their best work when supported by capable teammates in an organization that provides the proper tools and information to enable effective action. It is difficult for even the best people to operate competently if they are not provided with the proper support from their teams and organizations. Though it may be difficult or impossible to make an incompetent person operate competently, organizations should make sure that they do not hobble their best people by inattention to building competence at the team and organizational levels.

The Importance of Competency Assessments

It is silly car owners who do not take their cars to the dealer for scheduled checkups. During these checkups, the dealer puts the car through a diagnostic procedure, looking for trouble spots. If the car is declared "healthy," the owner can drive away from the dealer confident that the car will function properly into the near future. If a problem is identified, it can be fixed, and again the owner drives away confident of smooth driving.

So it is with project-based organizations. In these organizations, competency assessments should be carried out periodically to determine the health of the overall organization and its component parts. Project workers should be assessed according to their knowledge and understanding of good project management practices. Are they familiar with the rudiments of solid scheduling, budgeting, and resource allocation principles? Do they possess the people skills needed to work with their customers, managers, and teammates? Are they able to cope with the business side of projects? Chapter Eight provides a sample diagnostic exam that focuses on standard project management knowledge-based competencies. Project workers who take and pass the Project Management Institute's certification exam can make a prima facie case that they have mastered knowledge-related issues in project management. Of course this does not mean that they possess solid project competencies in the social and business arenas.

Teams should similarly be put through competency assessments. Are they working with clearly defined performance objectives? Do they have effective decision-making processes in place? Is a team discipline in place, as reflected in well-established methods and procedures? A team assessment checklist is offered in Chapter Ten.

Finally, the organization itself should undergo a competency assessment. Does it have information systems in place to provide project teams with the information they need to do their jobs effectively? Does it behave as a learning organization, continually adjusting itself to changing conditions both within and outside the organization? Does it support the learning of its workforce through education, training, and job enrichment? Does it offer its workers the human and material resources they need? An organizational assessment checklist is offered in Chapter Twelve.

Last Word

The economic world described by Adam Smith in *Wealth of Nations* ([1776] 1991) is finally upon us. Smith described the workings of a free marketplace in which business decisions on what to produce, how much to produce, and how to price products were guided by an "invisible hand." Smith's free market was an interesting construct, but the reality of the business environment in the ensuing two centuries fell short of the model. The fact is that economic production has been strongly influenced by the existence of monopolies, oligopolies, and government intervention right up to the present day.

The information and transportation revolutions, however, have led to a situation in which Smith's model is finally approaching reality. Because of global competition today, it is difficult for even the most powerful players to establish monopolies. (Microsoft Corporation is a notable exception.) Even government attempts to control business activity are defeated by economic forces that lie outside of the government's realm of action and control. With instant access to information, buyers and sellers can make informed judgments. In addition, with the existence of the Internet, wireless communications, cheap computing power, and other information-based technologies, even the smallest player has a chance to compete against the behemoths.

In this brutally competitive world, the advantage lies with the most competent players. Through their competence, they can get it right the first time and avoid costly mistakes. They can channel their energies into activities that lead to the highest returns and avoid unproductive ventures. They can know when to take risks and when to eschew them. Their competence inspires customers to have confidence in them and this leads to repeat business. We are living in a meritocracy in which the highest rewards go to the best performers.

Given this reality, it behooves individuals and organizations to do whatever they can to elevate their levels of competence. A key theme of this book is that this entails plenty of hard work. Competence is not a gift passed down from heaven. It must be earned.

References

Adams, S. *The Dilbert Principle.* New York: HarperCollins, 1996.

Allison, G. T. *The Essence of Decision.* Boston: Little, Brown, 1971.

Argyris, C. *Interpersonal Competence and Organizational Effectiveness.* Florence, Ky.: Dorsey Press, 1962.

Block, R. *The Politics of Projects.* New York: Yourdon Press, 1984.

Block, T., and Frame, J. D. *Project Office: A Key to Managing Projects Effectively.* Menlo Park, Calif.: Crisp, 1997.

Bolman, L. G., and Deal, T. E. *Reframing Organizations: Artistry, Choice, and Leadership.* (2nd ed.) San Francisco: Jossey-Bass, 1997.

Brooks, F. P., Jr. *The Mythical Man-Month: Essays on Software Engineering.* Reading, Mass.: Addison-Wesley, 1975.

Burrough, B. *Barbarians at the Gate.* New York: HarperCollins, 1990.

Byrne, J. A., Symonds, W. C., and Siler, J. F. "CEO Disease." *Business Week,* Apr. 1, 1991, pp. 52–59.

Cabanis, J. "I Was Born for It." *PM Network,* 1997, *11*(1), 26–28.

Carter, J. *Why Not the Best?* Nashville, Tenn.: Broadman Press, 1975.

Chopra, D. *The Seven Spiritual Laws of Success.* San Rafael, Calif.: New World Library, 1994.

Darwin, C. *On the Origin of Species by Means of Natural Selection.* New York: Avenel Books, 1979. (Originally published 1859.)

Darwin, C. *The Descent of Man, and Selection in Relation to Sex.* New York: New York University Press, 1989. (Originally published 1871.)

Drucker, P. F. *The Practice of Management.* New York: HarperCollins, 1954.

Drucker, P. F. *The Effective Executive.* New York: HarperCollins, 1967.

Duncan, W. R. "Project Management Standards Applications." *PM Network,* 1998, *12*(7), 17–18.

Duncan, W. R. (ed.). *Guide to the Project Management Body of Knowledge.* Upper Darby, Pa.: PMI Publications, 1996.

Frame, J. D. *Managing Projects in Organizations: How to Make the Best Use of Time, Techniques, and People.* (2nd ed.)San Francisco: Jossey-Bass, 1995.

Frame, J. D. *The New Project Management: Tools for an Age of Rapid Change, Corporate Reengineering, and Other Business Realities.* San Francisco: Jossey-Bass, 1994.

Gardner, H. *Frames of Mind: The Theory of Multiple Intelligences.* New York: Basic Books, 1983.

Gardner, J. W. *On Leadership.* New York: Free Press, 1989.

Goleman, D. *Emotional Intelligence: Why It Can Matter More Than IQ.* New York: Bantam Books, 1995.

Halal, W. E. *The New Management: Democracy and Enterprise Are Transforming Organizations.* San Francisco: Berrett-Koehler, 1996.

Handy, C. B. *The Age of Unreason.* Boston: Harvard Business School Press, 1989.

Handy, C. B. *The Age of Paradox.* Boston: Harvard Business School Press, 1994.

Hanon, M. *Consultative Selling.* New York: AMACOM, 1985.

Harvey, J. B. *The Abilene Paradox and Other Meditations.* San Francisco: Jossey-Bass, 1996.

Herrnstein, R. J. "I.Q." *Atlantic Monthly,* Sept. 1971, pp. 43–64.

Herrnstein, R. J., and Murray, C. *The Bell Curve.* New York: Free Press, 1994.

Herzberg, F. "One More Time: How Do You Motivate Employees?" *Harvard Business Review,* 1968, *46*(1), 53–63.

Jain, A. "Project Management Maturity Model: A New Outlook." Working paper, 1998.

James, W. *Pragmatism.* White Plains, N.Y.: Longman, 1907.

Jaques, E., and Cason, K. *Human Capability.* Falls Church, Va.: Cason Hall, 1994.

Jensen, A. R. "How Much Can We Boost IQ and Scholastic Achievement?" *Harvard Education Review,* 1969, *39,* 1–123.

Juran, J. M. *Juran on Planning for Quality.* New York: Free Press, 1988.

Katzenbach, J. R., and Smith, D. K. *The Wisdom of Teams.* Boston: Harvard Business School Press, 1993.

Kidder, T. *The Soul of a New Machine.* Boston: Little, Brown, 1981.

Kidder, T. *House.* Boston: Houghton Mifflin, 1985.

Kohn, A. "Why Incentive Plans Cannot Work." *Harvard Business Review,* 1993, *74*(5), 54–61.

Labarre, P. "This Organization Is Disorganization." *Fast Company,* June–July 1996.

Levin, G., Ward, J. L., and Hill, G. "Maturity Assessment: What Happens Using ProjectFRAMEWORK." *Project Management Horizons,* Oct. 1998, pp. 1–2.

Parkinson, C. N. *Parkinson's Law, and Other Studies in Administration.* New York: Ballantine, 1957.

Peter, L. J., and Hull, R. *The Peter Principle.* New York: Morrow, 1969.

Peters, T. *The Tom Peters Seminar.* New York: Random House, 1994.

Pinchot, G., and Pinchot, E. *The End of Bureaucracy and the Rise of the Intelligent Organization.* San Francisco: Berrett-Koehler, 1993.

Prahalad, C. K., and Hamel, G. "The Core Competence of the Organization." *Harvard Business Review,* 1990, *68*(3), 79–92.

Rayner, S. R. *Team Traps: Survival Stories from Team Disasters, Near-Misses, Mishaps, and Other Near-Death Experiences.* New York: Wiley, 1996.

Reich, R. B. *The Work of Nations: Preparing Ourselves for Twenty-First-Century Capitalism.* New York: Knopf, 1991.

Remy, R. "Adding Focus to Improvement Efforts with PM³." *PM Network,* July 1997, pp. 43–47.

Rich, B. R., and Janos, L. *Skunk Works: A Personal Memoir from the U-2 to the Stealth Fighter.* Boston: Little, Brown, 1994.

Schumpeter, J. A. *Capitalism, Socialism, and Democracy.* New York: Harper-Collins, 1950.

Senge, P. M. *The Fifth Discipline: The Art and Practice of the Learning Organization.* New York: Doubleday, 1990.

Shockley, W. "Jensen's Data on Spearman's Hypothesis: No Artifact." *Behavioral and Brain Sciences,* 1987, *10,* 512.

Shoda, Y., Mischel, W., and Peake, P. K. "Predicting Adolescent Cognitive and Self-Regulatory Competencies from Preschool Delay of Gratification." *Developmental Psychology,* 1990, *26*(6), 978–986.

Smith, A. *Wealth of Nations.* New York: Knopf, 1991. (Originally published 1776.)

Software Engineering Institute. *Capability Maturity Model for Software, Version 1.1, CMU/SEI-93-TR-24.* Pittsburgh: Carnegie Mellon University, 1993a.

Software Engineering Institute. *Key Practices for the Capability Maturity Model, Version 1.1, CMU/SEI-93-TR-25.* Pittsburgh: Carnegie Mellon University, 1993b.

Standish Group. *Chaos: Charting the Seas of Information Technology.* Dennis, Mass.: Standish Group International, 1994.

Stevenson, K. "Achieving Enhanced Effectiveness in the Management and Support of Projects: An Examination of Organisational Project Management Competence." Unpublished doctoral dissertation, University of South Queensland, Australia, 1998.

Stewart, T. A. "Navigating by Starlight: Career Guidance from the Class of 1970." *Fortune,* 1995a, *132*(3), 252ff.

Stewart, T. A. "Planning a Career in a World Without Managers." *Fortune,* 1995b, *31*(5), 72ff.

Tenner, A. R., and DeToro, I. J. *Total Quality Management: Three Steps to Continuous Improvement.* Reading, Mass.: Addison-Wesley, 1992.

Tyler, P. *Running Critical.* New York: HarperCollins, 1986.

Tzu, S. *The Art of War.* (S. B. Griffith, trans.). Oxford, England: Oxford University Press, 1963.

Vaill, P. B. *Managing as a Performing Art: New Ideas for a World of Chaotic Change.* San Francisco: Jossey-Bass, 1989.

Veblen, T. *Imperial Germany and the Industrial Revolution.* Old Tappan, N.J.: Macmillan, 1915.

Walters, J. M., and Gardner, H. "Multiple Intelligences." In R. J. Sternberg and R. K. Wagner (eds.), *Practical Intelligence.* Cambridge, England: Cambridge University Press, 1986.

Weber, M. *The Theory of Social and Economic Organization.* (T. Parsons, ed.). Oxford, England: Oxford University Press, 1947.

Weinberg, G. *The Psychology of Computer Programming.* New York: Van Nostrand Reinhold, 1971.

Wellins, R. S., Byham, W. C., and Wilson, J. M. *Empowered Teams: Creating Self-Directed Work Groups That Improve Quality, Productivity, and Participation.* San Francisco: Jossey-Bass, 1991.

Wilson, P. F., and Pearson, R. D. *Performance-Based Assessments: External, Internal, and Self-Assessment Tools for Total Quality Management.* Milwaukee, Wis.: American Society for Quality Control Press, 1995.

Index